WON'T CREATE
SMAR

To becoming more
expert in
learning &
teaching —

Eric Haas

DUMB IDEAS
WON'T CREATE
SMART KIDS

Straight Talk About Bad School Reform, Good Teaching, and Better Learning

Eric M. Haas, Gustavo E. Fischman, and Joe Brewer

Foreword by George Lakoff

TEACHERS
COLLEGE
PRESS

Teachers College, Columbia University
New York and London

Published by Teachers College Press, 1234 Amsterdam Avenue, New York, NY
10027

Library of Congress Cataloging-in-Publication Data is available from www.loc.gov

Haas, Eric (Eric M.)
   Dumb ideas won't create smart kids : straight talk about bad school reform,
     good teaching, and better learning / Eric M. Haas, Gustavo E. Fischman, &
     Joe Brewer ; foreword by George Lakoff.
       pages cm
   Includes bibliographical references and index.
   ISBN 978-0-8077-5553-2 (pbk. : alk. paper)
   ISBN 978-0-8077-7321-5 (ebook)
     1. School improvement programs. I. Fischman, Gustavo. II. Title.
   LB2822.8.H33   2014
   371.2'07—dc23   2014010982

ISBN 978-0-8077-5553-2 (paper)
ISBN 978-0-8077-7321-5 (ebook)

Printed on acid-free paper
Manufactured in the United States of America

21   20   19   18   17   16   15   14   8   7   6   5   4   3   2   1

Contents

We want to dedicate this book to all of our former, current, and future students and teachers

This book is our humble attempt to say thank you and repay our debts for all that we have gained from the many people who have guided us over the years. With gratitude for all of your support, encouragement, and insights, we note especially:

Gary Anderson, David C. Berliner, Pat Brewer, Norman Fairclough, Gene V Glass, Liesl Haas, Rich Haesly, Kathryn Herr, Alfred Hübler, George Lakoff, Jessica Lisiewski, Leslie Poynor, Michaela Poynor-Haas, Jeanne Powers, Sandra R. Sales, Rose Sherman, and Amy Topper

Foreword

This is an important book, perhaps the most important book you will read on the nature of education. It tells deep and vital truths. It tells you many things that you need to know.

Much of what is called educational "reform" does not work. It fails because it is based on false assumptions. What is scary is that these false assumptions arise naturally. The assumptions may seem right at first glance. But they are false, and they are harmful. You don't see bacteria and viruses, but they can harm you and your kids. Similarly, you may not be aware of the unconscious ideas you've inherited, but they are there and they can be disastrous.

Let's begin with some brain basics. All thought is physical. Thought is carried out by brain circuitry. Much of that circuitry is learned early in life, and may not change easily, if at all. And you can only understand what your brain allows you to understand. To learn certain truths, your brain may have to change first. That is why this book exists. To understand how education actually works, you may have to change some false assumptions first.

Most of thought is unconscious, effortless, and fast. A common estimate is about 98%, more or less. Conscious thought is the tip of the iceberg, and it is effortful and slow. But we need to use it to understand what is unconscious.

Much of unconscious thought is metaphorical in nature, and many of those metaphors are simply taken as truths. For example, when Michael Reddy was teaching at Columbia Teachers College back in 1977, he read a study on social policy by Donald Schön of MIT, in which Schön observed that when things go wrong, people often use their most common unconscious metaphors for comprehending what is going wrong, and they may act on those metaphors. Reddy, teaching composition in the English Department, was very much concerned with communication. To discover what he and his fellow professors assumed about communication, he collected his colleagues' comments on freshman essays, comments like "Try to get your thoughts across better" and "Pack more thoughts into fewer words," and so on, with hundreds of examples. The comments showed the most common metaphorical mode of thinking about communication, what Reddy called the *conduit metaphor*: Ideas Are Objects, Words Are Containers for Ideas, Communication Is Sending the Idea-Objects in the Language-Containers. It is a mode of understanding that is used constantly and taken as a truth.

But, as Reddy pointed out, it is false. It assumes that communication is the responsibility of the speaker: put the ideas in the right words and the hearer will take those same ideas out and put them in her head. Teaching on this metaphor is just transferring ideas from one mind to another. The minds of children are assumed to be *empty vessels*, and teaching is filling up those vessels with the ideas you are transferring. By measuring how many of those ideas make it into the empty vessels, you can determine how effective a teacher is. It seems obvious. None of it is true.

At any age, you can only understand what your brain allows you to understand. You are born with about 100 billion neurons and close to a quadrillion connections between them. Through experience, the connections used are strengthened and those unused die off. By age 5, close to half of those connections have died off, shaping the brain, making some things easy to learn and other things hard if not impossible—different things for different children. Different children's brain are shaped in different ways *outside* of school, in homes and communities, and 5-years-olds come to school with elaborate ways of unconsciously understanding their worlds. New understandings are based on the brain circuitry already there. Learning requires growth, especially learning how to learn and how to think. Active learning is constructing, and often reconstructing, an understanding of the world. Each child arrives at school with a different, already shaped, unconsciously functioning brain. Teaching is nurturing each of those brains. It is anything but transferring the same fixed ideas into a bunch of empty vessels. The Conduit metaphor and the Empty Vessel metaphor stand in the way of effective teaching that nurtures growth in each individual child.

Education is essential to democracy, and not merely because civics and civic responsibility have to be taught. Education is fundamentally about freedom. If you are not educated, you are not free. First, you will lack the knowledge and skills to function effectively in a free society. Second, you will not be aware of the opportunities for fulfillment in life. Third, you will not be free to participate meaningfully in creating and maintaining the conditions for freedom through citizenship. Fourth, you will not be knowledgeable enough to become and stay healthy, and without health you cannot be free.

It is a central truth of a democratic society that the private depends on the public, that is, on all the resources that the public provides for all. It begins with protection—not just public safety and a justice system, but protection of food, air, and water, protection from poisons in our environment, and protections from fraud and harmfully unfair treatment and oppression. But it goes on to vast ranges of opportunity. You can't run a business without such public provisions as sewers, roads and bridges, publicly provided airports and shipping facilities, and public research developments like the internet, satellite communication, pharmaceuticals—and especially public education at all levels. Even private education depends on the public. Private universities are very largely funded by public research, private companies make use of publicly developed patents, and many private companies depend on public contracts, public subsidies, and the use of publicly owned resources, whether airwaves, grazing lands, or mineral leases. And at the heart of all of this is public education!

Understanding the fallacies of the Conduit and Empty Vessel metaphors—and remedying those fallacies—is no small matter. From the perspective of the fabric of life in a democracy, what happens in schools is of major concern to all of us. That is why this book is important.

—George Lakoff

Introduction

If you are reading this book, it is very likely that you work in education, and so both within and outside your work, people probably need or want to know your opinion about the latest reforms. What's your reaction when somebody asks for your opinion about how schools and students are doing? How do you feel about reports about the poor achievement of U.S. students, from low international rankings among industrialized nations on the Programme for International Assessment (PISA) test (Organization for Economic Co-operation and Development [OECD], 2013a)[1] to graduation rates of only 62% and 51% among African American and Native American students, respectively (Swanson & Lloyd, 2013),[2] to percentages of college freshmen taking remedial courses as high as 40% in Ohio (Ohio Board of Regents, 2013) and 51% in New Mexico (New Mexico Higher Education Department, 2014)?

Which education reforms first came to your mind when you saw "Dumb Ideas" in the title of our book? What do you say when a family member wants to know your ideas about the new Race to the Top reform, the Common Core State Standards, computerized standardized tests, using test scores as significant factors in teacher and principal evaluation, and laws that encourage the rapid growth of charter schools? What is your opinion about other reforms, such as alternative teacher certification and longer school days? How do you react when you are first approached to work on these issues as part of a school, district, state, or national committee to improve student achievement?

Some of the typical responses we encountered are:

"These changes are wonderful. It's about time."
"Idiotic. It will never work."
"Yuck. It's unfair."
"Of course. Duh."
"What a dumb idea!"
"What a smart idea!"

You might respond with some mixture of all of these responses, perhaps, depending on the issue, the context of the inquiry (at a committee meeting, your kid's soccer game, or a family holiday dinner), and the time (before or after coffee)? If you are like us, regardless of the issue, the context, and the time, you had an immediate, gut reaction to the student performance results and those education reforms.

You cannot prevent having gut reactions (Kahneman, 2011), but in general we try to explain our perspectives by using rational arguments and supporting evidence.[3] In this case, how much have you deliberately thought about the evidence for how well the Common Core State Standards, computerized standardized tests, student test scores in teacher and principal evaluation, charter schools, alternative teacher certification programs, extended school days, or any other reform idea will contribute to improving student achievement? Perhaps a lot. Perhaps some or not much. We agree with the general consensus that choosing education reforms should be based on evidence of the likelihood of their success (see, e.g., Whitehurst, 2009; Zucker, 2004),[4] but educators rarely, if ever, have the time or resources to develop "perfect knowledge" on the likely success of every education reform possibility. So the issue really becomes, what do we accept as sufficient evidence that a possible education reform will be successful? How do we make that determination? And ultimately, how well are we doing in identifying, promoting, and implementing effective or likely to be effective education reforms? In sum, how can we develop both our fast gut reactions and our slow deliberations so that they can work together to enable us to consistently recognize which education ideas are smart ones—those supported by credible evidence of likely success—and which are dumb ones—those not supported by credible evidence of likely success?

Let's unpack some of the dynamics between our initial gut reactions, our rational arguments, and what is credible evidence by beginning to examine two current education reforms: implementing the Common Core State Standards and expanding National Board Certification for teachers.

To start, what is your initial reaction when you see people promoting the Common Core State Standards or National Board Certification as a way to improve student achievement, such as being ready for college or career, among other possible student outcomes? Take a moment to think about that. If you had to state right now whether either would be successful in improving student achievement, what would you say? Would you support either one? Neither? Both?

Now, think about how well you know the evidence for or against the Common Core State Standards and National Board Certification for teachers. What kinds of evidence were you thinking about? Randomized controlled trial quantitative studies? Qualitative observations of classrooms and schools? Interviews or surveys with teachers, parents, or students? Your own experience as a student, parent, educator, or policymaker? At this moment, how well can you explain the extent of the evidence you considered or the moment when you felt that you had enough of the right evidence to decide whether to support or reject these reforms?

Support for "evidence-based policy" and trust in the value of scientific evidence is widespread (Nutley et al., 2000, 2007), explicitly defended by researchers as well as government officers, ministers and advisors, senior civil servants, local school board members, and principals (Luke, Green, & Kelly, 2010). But this widespread consensus often masks two issues: (1) There is no conclusive universal consensus about what counts as "scientific" evidence (Erickson, 2014; Liebow et al., 2013) nor one that could, by itself, automatically generate predominant support in favor of any given educational policy decision; and (2) any type of "evidence," be it empirical or conceptual, collected by quantitative or qualitative methods, cannot avoid entering into the realm of policy debates through multiple processes of interpretation and contextualization that often alter the compelling quality of the collected "evidence." In short, there is no such thing as pure factual evidence that is objectively persuasive, because all evidence comes with a frame for interpretation (Dumas & Anderson, 2014; Luke, Green, & Kelly, 2010). In other words, what people determine to be persuasive evidence depends on the proposed reform, the context of where and when the reform will be implemented, and the individual understandings, including the gut reactions, of the people making the decision (Fischman & Tefera, 2014).

When reading any major newspaper or blog about education, it is very clear that politicians, researchers, and the public have very strong and polarized opinions and perspectives about what works and what should be done to fix education (Bennett, 2013; Haas & Fischman, 2010). Each side attacks the other using several strategies, but two of the most common and related ones are "Are you stupid? This [my idea] is just common sense," which is often complemented with the second strategy of "your evidence is not as strong as mine" (compare Polikoff, 2014; Ravitch, 2013a, 2013b; Sawchuk, 2014). Yet, how can we fiercely defend our perspectives and try to reach agreements when we don't even have a shared understanding of how to define strong evidence of support, including how and when supporting evidence is and should be persuasive that a policy idea is likely to be successful (Lakoff, 2002, 2008)? As we will explain throughout the book, our perspectives are highly influenced by our initial "gut" reactions. These reactions should be expected, as they are natural, automatic responses brought on by the unconscious brain at work (Kahneman, 2011). Psychologist Daniel Kahneman, winner of the 2002 Nobel Prize in Economics, describes two interwoven and interactive levels of thinking: "thinking fast" (the unconscious level of initial gut reactions) and "thinking slow" (the conscious level of deliberate, self-guided thought).[5] Harvard psychologist Joshua Greene (2013) describes these two types of thinking in terms of a camera on "automatic mode" (unconscious level) and "manual mode" (conscious level), while New York University psychology professor Jonathan Haidt (2006) describes them as an elephant (our emotional unconscious side) and its rider (our conscious rational side). What Kahneman and Greene, among others, including Ariely (2008, 2010), Churchland (2013), Gibbs (2008), Haidt (2012), Heath and Heath (2010), Lakoff (2002, 2008), and LeDoux (2003), have shown is that each level of consciousness has an important role in our thinking and the success of our everyday decisionmaking. Further, when we work to get our unconscious and conscious thinking in sync regarding a particular topic, we can become more successful, even "expert" (Lemov, Woolway, Yezzi, & Heath, 2012; Lindon, 2013), in achieving good results. At the same time, our unconscious and conscious thinking can also act in opposition, pushing us toward a panacea in line with our gut reaction, rather than an evidence-based solution (Heath & Heath, 2010). So, managing the positives and shortcomings of our fast and slow thinking is important to becoming more successful at anything, including decisions about which education reforms are most likely to be effective in improving student achievement, among other student outcomes.

In sum, our automatic reactions to a reform and the challenges of knowing the most relevant evidence about each reform create some dilemmas about identifying and promoting education reforms that will likely be successful. It seems problematic, but not infrequent, to just follow our automatic fast reactions, simply presuming that they are accurate (Ariely, 2008, 2010). At the same time, we rarely have the time or resources to develop perfect knowledge (even assuming that can be done). So it does not seem very productive to attempt to just slow down, aiming to achieve idealized, perfect knowledge each time we must decide something about education, including the daily implementation decisions across all contexts in the United States. It seems that we must somehow find a smarter way to harness both our automatic fast-thinking reactions and our deliberate slow-thinking examination of evidence in identifying, promoting, and implementing education reforms. That is the intent of this book.

Let's return to our examination of the Common Core State Standards and National Board Certification to address how well we are doing in identifying, promoting, and implementing effective or likely to be effective education reforms. What evidence do we have that these reform ideas will improve student achievement and enable today's students to be successful in tomorrow's world? And, how does the level of evidence align with the reforms' popularity as ideas? (We will discuss both reform ideas in more detail in Chapter 5.) If they don't align, what might explain the discrepancy? Should we be concerned? And, if so, what can we do about that?

We start with the Common Core State Standards (CCSS). As with most educational proposals, there is some disagreement about whether standards are effective in raising student achievement; however, the preponderance of the evidence appears to be that they are not. For example, Morgan Polikoff (2014), an assistant professor at the University of Southern California, writes in support of the CCSS, stating that there is a "fairly reasonable research base" that content standards influence teachers' instruction and that standards, *combined with accountability threats on schools and teachers*, have, in some situations, led to changes in teacher practice that have boosted student learning.[6] In contrast, the late education professor Gerald Bracey (2009) and current Brown University professor and former head of the Institute of Education Science at the U.S. Department of Education Russ Whitehurst (2009) directly examined the relationship between state standards and student achievement and concluded the exact opposite.

After comparing NAEP and TIMSS scores to analyses of the quality of state standards, Gerald Bracey (2009) showed that there is "no evidence . . . that the simple act of raising standards or making them uniform across states will, in fact, cause increased student learning" (pp. 17–18). Russ Whitehurst (2009) examined the relationship between state math standards and student math achievement and concluded that there is

> virtually no relation between the level at which a state sets its standard and the mathematics achievement of its students. . . .
>
> The lack of evidence that better content standards enhance student achievement is remarkable given the level of investment in this policy and high hopes attached to it. There is a rational argument to be made for good content standards being a precondition for other desirable reforms, but it is currently just that—an argument. (p. 8)

Despite the lack of evidence that raising state standards will increase student achievement, the Common Core State Standards are a centerpiece of the Obama Administration's Race to the Top initiative and they have been adopted by 45 states and the District of Columbia (Common Core State Standards Initiative, 2014).

Why would U.S. and state policymakers put so much energy into a reform with so little, if any, evidence of effectiveness?

Now we examine National Board Certification. National Board Certification is an advanced teaching credential. To earn the credential, teachers must analyze their teaching context and students' needs, submit videos of their teaching, and provide work samples that demonstrate their students' growth and achievement. The reflective analyses that they submit must demonstrate:

1. A strong command of content;
2. The ability to design appropriate learning experiences that advance student learning;
3. The use of assessments to inform instructional decisionmaking; and
4. Partnerships with colleagues, parents, and the community. (National Board for Professional Teaching Standards, 2013a)

Through this structured and iterative process, teachers expand and refine their content knowledge and pedagogy. According to the National Board for Professional Teaching Standards (NBPTS) website, the outcome is more powerful teaching that improves student achievement and reflects college and career readiness.[7] Studies have consistently confirmed this conclusion, finding that the students of National Board Certified teachers (NBCTs) outperform the students of non-NBCTs (see, e.g., National Research Council, 2008; Vandervoort, Amrein-Beardsley, & Berliner, 2004).[8] Despite this evidence of success, only about 100,000 of the current 3 million teachers are National Board certified.[9] Further, there is no provision for increasing the number of National Board Certified teachers in the Race to the Top initiative, nor could we find any provisions to do so in any state reform efforts.

Why do U.S. and state policy-makers seem to ignore the consistent evidence of the positive impact of National Board Certification?

It seems clear to us that the popularity of the Common Core State Standards rather than National Board Certification as the means to improve student achievement shows that there is more to education reform decisionmaking than the conscious weighing of evidence. Evidence is necessary, of course, but it is not sufficient. And it is important to explain our position regarding the complex issue of what counts as "evidence" (Philips, 2014). As we've already stated, empirical evidence is necessary for choosing effective education reforms, and we are always in favor of analyzing the best existing empirical and conceptual sources of evidence. At the same time, we want to make two warnings against the presumed supremacy of empiricism. First, we take an expanded view of what is sound empirical evidence that can warrant the likelihood of the success of an education reform (Berliner, 2002b; Fischman & Tefera, 2014).[10]

Second, and more important, our example of the Common Core and National Board Certification illustrates that evidence, whether understood broadly or narrowly, does not reign supreme in the education decisionmaking process. People can and should place the gathering and weighing of evidence as a primary means for identifying and promoting education reforms, but that is not enough. We must do more than just recite evidence if we are going to identify and promote good education reforms, avoid bad ones, and convince others to do the same. Besides our previous example comparing the Common Core State Standards and National Board Certification, our own experiences talking politics at the family holiday dinner or watching public reaction to a presidential debate should tell us that evidence cannot be counted on as a persuasion silver bullet.

So, what can we do? Let's return to our initial automatic fast reactions to the list of current education reforms at the beginning of the chapter. We contend that our fast automatic and unconscious reactions are a strong, but not sufficiently acknowledged, influence that impacts our rational and conscious decisions about which education reforms we decide to promote, what evidence we find convincing, and even whether we need any evidence at all (Fischman & Haas, 2012). However, managing our fast and slow thinking is easier said than done. Our fast thinking is unconscious—which means that we must actively work on understanding how fast thinking influences slow thinking if we are to maximize the strengths and minimize the weaknesses of both in our education thinking. Successfully managing our slow and fast thinking in order to achieve goals is now understood in current psychology and neuroscience research as the essence of expertise (Camerer, Loewenstein, & Prelec, 2005; Haier & Jung, 2008; Heath & Heath, 2010; Kahneman, 2011; Sawyer, 2011), which for us is expertise in education thinking.

We propose that one of the key aspects for managing our thinking is an understanding of the automatic creation and use of models or frames of how the world works by our fast-thinking unconscious, which derive from our individual life experiences (Feldman, 2008; Gibbs, 2008; Goffman, 1986; Lakoff, 1987; Varela, Thompson, & Rosch, 1991). Specifically, we focus on the metaphors and prototypes that are a foundational part of these models or frames (Lakoff & Johnson, 2003; Prinz, 2002; Rosch, 1978). In brief, with more explanation in Chapters 1, 2, and 4, metaphors and prototypes are key aspects of these models or frames because they enable us to understand complex ideas in terms of more concrete ones. For example, nearly everyone has created a metaphor for understanding the concept of a "life" by idealizing it as a "journey" (Lakoff & Johnson, 2003), and we all create primary prototypes in order to understand groups of multicharacteristic things, such understanding "bachelor" as a prototype of someone like James Bond, but not the Pope (Prinz, 2002). Further, metaphors and prototypes include both a descriptive and a judgmental aspect to them; they tell us not only how the world works, but how it *should* work (Lakoff, 1987, 2002; Prinz, 2002). We do the same model and frame creation for understanding education, including metaphors for learning and prototypes for what schools or classroom are and what teachers and students look like and how they should behave (see, e.g., Botha, 2009; Haas & Fischman, 2010). This model or frame creation, including metaphors and prototypes, is how we learn (Clark, 2013; Gibbs, 2008), and we continually and automatically use the ones we have created to operate in the world (Lakoff & Johnson, 2003). As a result, they have a profound and continual influence not just on our fast thinking, but also on our slow thinking (Lakoff, 2002, 2008). Thus, the better we understand the metaphors and prototypes of our fast thinking in education, the better we can understand, develop, and manage our fast-thinking gut reactions and their influence on our slow-thinking deliberations.

We believe that policymakers, like most other people, have automatically created certain metaphors and prototypes about education that makes them predisposed at the fast-thinking level to believe that reforms such as raising standards will be more likely to improve student achievement than improving teacher expertise, regardless of what the evidence shows. Further, some metaphors and prototypes about education are more dominant than others, contributing to the development of a common sense or "educationalese" that operates mostly at the fast-thinking level (Fischman & Haas, 2012; Fischman & Tefera, 2014; Haas & Fischman, 2010). Educationalese tilts us toward seeing some policies and proposals as inherently better and others as inherently worse before we ever activate our slow thinking (Kumashiro, 2008, 2012). As we discussed with the disconnect between the evidence of effectiveness and the popularity of the CCSS and National Board Certification, educationalese can lead us to disregard evidence. This happens mostly because our fast-thinking reaction leads us to conclude that existing proposals are either working or inhibits our ability to imagine that alternatives might work better, making it seem unnecessary to consider contrary arguments and evidence (Fischman & Haas, 2012; Fischman & Tefera, 2014; Haas & Fischman, 2010). If our fast-thinking models were always accurate, then there would be no issue here, but as Kahneman (2011) documents, they are often not.

As a result, we must take an expanded approach in our education decisionmaking, one that directly confronts the influence of our unconscious, gut-level reactions in our thinking process and acknowledge that our fast thinking can lead us to consciously support ineffective ideas. We label this process as *rightly wrong* thinking.[11] *Rightly wrong* thinking feels right to our unconscious fast thinking, and we often justify our conclusions with a post hoc logical set of arguments to support what our gut has already told us must be right (Haidt, 2012).[12] We are not saying that *rightly wrong* thinking is the only explanation for supporting CCSS and not National Board Certification, or any other education reform. Clear and intentional economic interests, political rationales, and ideological preferences also play a big role for individuals and organizations who are promoting policies in the absence of evidence or in direct contradiction to what the preponderance of the evidence suggests (Arbesman, 2012; Kahneman, 2011).[13] Nevertheless, in our experience, *rightly wrong* thinking is a common and powerful influence shaping discussions about topics and issues, especially those that touch our emotions; in educational issues, these are abundant and difficult to change.

In this book we describe the importance of paying close attention to our fast and slow modes of thinking when making decisions about education reforms because we need to stop pretending that our fast, automatic, unconscious reactions, or the natural tension that we feel between our more emotional fast-thinking and our more deliberate slow-thinking modes of understanding, does not matter for educational reform decisions. Rather, our fast determination of whether an education reform is smart or dumb depends as much, if not more, on the prototypes and metaphors in our fast thinking than on the evidence we ponder in our slow thinking.

The example about the Common Core State Standards and National Board Certification, as well as many others that will be analyzed in later chapters, motivated us to write this book around a central idea. We can't avoid using our fast-thinking mode when discussing and analyzing educational proposals, but neither can we rely solely on fast thinking to make good decisions. Careful and "slow" (as Kahneman defines it) examination of evidence—formulating warranted and reasoned perspectives—is absolutely necessary as part of any effective decisionmaking process (Churchland, 2013; Greene, 2013; Kahneman, 2011). For example, policy decisions and long-term planning by groups such as government committees, school faculties, and parent organizations, as well as individual plans by parents and students, should involve the slow consideration of evidence, given that there is time, usually by design, to do so. In addition, conscious slow thinking can provide a check to our unconscious thinking and also contribute to training our unconscious to be more accurate (Churchland, 2013; Greene, 2013; Kahneman, 2011). The latter is especially important, because sometimes the reactions from our fast thinking are too strong to be overcome by our conscious slow examination of contradictory evidence (Heath & Heath, 2010). Of course, sometimes we have to think quickly on our feet and rely on our unconscious, fast thinking when we don't have the luxury of extended periods of time to fully examine the available evidence. For example, teachers in a classroom or people answering questions posed by education committee members must be able to think quickly on their feet and are thus forced to rely more on their fast-thinking reactions than they would if they had hours, days, or months to gather and ponder the available evidence. Or there simply is no evidentiary consensus and so we must be guided in large part on our unconscious fast reaction plus general conscious reasoning. The bottom line is this: If we are to be more successful at choosing education reforms, we must consider and, as much as possible, align our fast and slow decisionmaking processes. That is what this book is about.

We start this process in the next chapter by describing the current educationalese or predominant way that learning and teaching are understood using the CONDUIT metaphor for communication, the EMPTY VESSEL metaphor for the mind, and prototypes of homogeneity for teachers, students, and classrooms. In Chapter 2 we examine the influence of the current educationalese on current policies promoted by Michelle Rhee and her organization, StudentsFirst, as an example of the limitations of our current thinking about education reform and why a change is needed. In Chapter 3 we describe the latest research and knowledge about how we learn new ideas, and what types of teaching and learning activities will enable students to master important 21st-century skills, such as problem solving, open inquiry, collaboration, and knowledge integration. The latest research and knowledge about learning and expertise point out the inaccuracies and thus the limitations of the current educationalese built on the CONDUIT and EMPTY VESSEL metaphors and the homogeneity prototypes. Then, in Chapter 4, we describe a more accurate metaphor for understanding learning: the GROWTH metaphor. In Chapter 5, we will explore how using the GROWTH metaphor can enable us to more accurately understand learning and teaching, which can make us more effective at teaching students and at persuading policymakers, educators, and parents to move education policy and practice in the right direction. We present our final summary of key points in the conclusion in Chapter 6.

CHAPTER 1

The Metaphors and Prototypes of the Predominant Fast-Thinking Educationalese

As we began to describe in the Introduction, we are not blank slates about the physical world, nor about the social and political issues of our day (Lakoff, 1987, 2002). Rather, over the course of our individual, everyday lived experiences, we have automatically developed models and frames of how the world works, which form the basis of our fast thinking. This process of developing understandings of the world based on our physical experience living in it is referred to as *embodied cognition* (Feldman, 2008; Gibbs, 2008; Iacaboni, 2008; Varela, Thompson, & Rosch, 1991). That is, we learn to understand and effectively function in the world not just when somebody is explicitly trying to teach us something, but also and even more frequently when we automatically and mostly unconsciously develop models of how the world works through the living out of our lives.

Further, we establish priorities not by a detached, exclusively conscious, slow-thinking process, but by a complex interaction between our fast and slow thinking, where our fast thinking plays a fundamental role. Camerer, Loewenstein, and Prelec (2005) describe the influences of our fast thinking (which they label as automatic, affective, and below consciousness) and slow thinking (which they label as conscious, cognitive deliberation, and controlled) on our thinking and decisionmaking processes:

> Human behavior thus requires a fluid interaction between controlled and automatic processes, and between cognitive and affective systems. However, many behaviors that emerge from this interplay are routinely and falsely interpreted as being the product of cognitive deliberation alone (Wolford, Miller, & Gazzaniga 2000). These results . . . suggest that introspective accounts of the basis for choice should be taken with a grain of salt. Because automatic

processes are designed to keep behavior "off-line" and below consciousness, we have far more introspective access to controlled than to automatic processes. Since we see only the top of the automatic iceberg, we naturally tend to exaggerate the importance of control. (p. 11)

That's how our minds function in the real world. And, as we will repeat throughout this book, these models do not have to be accurate; they just have to "work" for us in some basic way. A model works when it enables us to provide a functional explanation or process in our circumstance. Sometimes, this means that a model works when a task is completed successfully—like baking a cake or changing a flat tire—where the accuracy of knowledge aligns clearly with a desired outcome. Other times, it means that a model works when a psychological concern has been addressed, as when a threatening idea—such as global warming or racial prejudice in the United States—has been dismissed as implausible because it creates anxiety in the mind of the person (Arbesman, 2012; Karafiath & Brewer, 2013; Lakoff, 2002, 2008; Schulz, 2010). These models influence our behaviors at both our fast- and slow-thinking levels to "work" in subtle and often counterintuitive ways. And, when the model we created is internally logical, but actually inaccurate, we have *rightly wrong* thinking. We will keep coming back to this point in our examples throughout the rest of this book.

In education, it is safe to say that everyone in the United States knows what *school* is—that is, at least on the fast-thinking level, we have some models or frames for understanding all things *school* (Goffman, 1986). Each person's models will be accurate (or inaccurate) to different degrees, but we all have them. You can't live in the United States without picking up some understanding of *school*, either directly as a student, and also possibly as a parent or educator, or indirectly through the way movies, television, the Internet, and our friends and relatives depict school. From all these experiences, as well as possibly some conscious instruction and thought, we know automatically what the words *teacher, student, classroom*, and *test* mean, along with a long list of other terms related to education. When we walk into a classroom, we have a fast-thinking sense of who the teacher is; who the students are; what the books, desks, whiteboard, and any computers are for; and how everyone should be acting.

Along with the more physical aspects of school, we also have created some fast-thinking ideas about the more amorphous aspects of education, such as how learning happens, what being smart or dumb looks like, and what is fair or unfair in school settings, among others. We have developed models for these concepts the same way that we developed our models and frames about the more physical aspects of schooling: through our direct experiences with schools and with our indirect interactions with media representations of schooling and the stories that other people share about their experiences with school. And to the degree that we have similar direct and indirect experiences with education and schooling, we develop many similar fast-thinking understandings, and also some slow ones.

Prototypes, Metaphors, and Educationalese

In this chapter, we describe the currently predominant fast-thinking understandings—the educationalese—that many people have about education and schooling. Through a couple of reflection activities, we will begin to describe the predominant metaphors and prototypes that make up our fast-thinking understanding, as well as how they influence our slow thinking. And we will transition into the next chapter with an example of how the current educationalese of predominant fast-thinking metaphors and prototypes that we describe can lead us to an example of *rightly wrong* thinking: the active, conscious promotion of certain education reforms despite strong evidence that they are likely ineffective. Then in Chapters 3 and 4 we will examine in more depth the research on how metaphors and prototypes develop and operate as part of the process of learning in order to develop a plan for aligning our fast and slow thinking to become more expert at choosing effective educational programs and reforms.

Let's start to understand the current educationalese by examining aspects of our education experience and the models, including the predominant metaphors and prototypes, of education that resulted from them by doing two activities.

For the first activity, quickly think of a high school math class. If you can, make a fast drawing right now on a piece of scrap paper. Do it in 45 seconds. If not, imagine drawing one. Go.

What does it look like? Is it a room with about 20–30 kids in rows of individual desks? Is there a teacher standing near a whiteboard (or chalkboard) at the front of the room with some information on it? Are the kids looking at textbooks or some type of worksheet? Are all the kids the same age?

If you did think of something like this, then you are in the vast majority of the people with whom we've done this activity—teachers, district administrators, university faculty, students, and parents. Nearly everyone draws the same thing when they have to quickly draw a class because this requires you to put down what first comes to your mind. This is, essentially, your unconscious prototype of what a high school math class is and probably what you think it should be.

Prototypes have a very strong influence on our thinking, even though most people do not consciously realize it unless they have been trained to be aware of them (Lakoff, 1987; Murphy, 2002; Prinz, 2002; Varela, Thompson, & Rosch, 1991). To see an example of a prototype's influence, look back at the task you just did. We asked you to draw a class, not a classroom. Nevertheless, nearly everyone draws a school classroom. No one with whom we have done this activity so far has drawn anything else. For example, no one has drawn students looking at an online video math lesson at home. Not a single person has drawn students out measuring something in their neighborhood or students giving their neighbors a survey that they will later analyze. No one has drawn an internship where someone is using math as part of his or her work. No one has drawn a hands-on tech activity, like students using math to determine how to alter the engine compartment to convert a hybrid car into a plug-in car. In fact, most people draw something that is similar to what they did most often in school.

Why is this response so consistent from all of these people? The short answer is that people are representing their own experiences, and most of those experiences are very similar. The experience that most people have had throughout their K–12 schooling, and often into college, involves sitting in classrooms receiving information from a teacher and doing mostly individual work in their seats, like taking notes or doing problems similar to the ones that the teacher just did at the front of the class. If you are like most people, from years and years of experiencing a class as a classroom of students in rows and a teacher disseminating information, you have constructed in your mind that this is what a high school class(room) is—in other words, a *prototype*.

The drawing of a class as a classroom did not have to turn out this way. We could have had another prototype of a class in our minds. Nearly everyone could have automatically envisioned a hands-on classroom where students are working in groups at tables on some type of project with a teacher or teachers moving around the room and helping the various groups as each needs it. The students could have been of multiple ages as well. Perhaps the classroom could have been something other than a room—perhaps kids in a field doing some type of research for a science or math class or in a city neighborhood doing a student-designed survey on political views for a history or social studies class. But practically no one envisions classes like these because most people have experienced the same basic type of schooling when they were students. So have all of their friends and family members. And they probably see this same type of schooling daily in the media. So we automatically and unconsciously construct this idea of what a classroom is without ever being taught or told to do so. This construction process is an example of embodied cognition: We learn to understand the world by automatically creating unconscious models based on the information we receive through our senses as we go about our daily lives.

Now, let's do the second activity. Please take a look at Figures 1.1 and 1.2. What do you see? Are there any familiar patterns? Anything surprising? Any detail that grabs your attention?

Figure 1.1. Photo of Earliest Known Example of a School, an Assyrian Classroom Circa 2000 B.C.

Source: Cole, M. (2010). What's Culture Got to Do with It? Educational Research as a Necessarily Interdisciplinary Enterprise. *Educational Researcher, 39*(6), 461–470, p. 463. Copyright © 2010 by Michael Cole. Reprinted by permission of SAGE Publications.

Figure 1.2. Miss Logan in Ohio State Normal College Model School Classroom, 1911

Source: Miami University Library, photo by Frank R. Snyder, available at digital. lib.miamioh.edu/u?/snyder,4100

When we show these images in workshop and classroom settings, most people answered that they are both photographs of a "classroom." And, they are. The first photograph is of an Assyrian classroom from around 2000 B.C. The second photograph is from a model school in Ohio in 1911. Often people also respond, especially when they look at the second photograph of the Ohio model school, that this is what good teaching and learning should look like: one teacher explaining some topic to a group of students who are attentively listening or individually working on some assigned task. With minor variations around this central theme, these images contain all the elements that have dominated our understanding and imagination about learning from ancient times until today. These are, in essence, examples of a prototype we have of *school* or *classroom*, as well as the related concepts of what *teaching* and *learning* do, and even should, look like. Education, as understood through these prototypes, can be reduced to the following equation: Teacher Delivering Prepackaged Information to Students = Education.

These two images most likely looked very similar to the classroom you drew or imagined in the previous activity. Not much has changed in education practice during all of this time, and so neither have our related fast-thinking education models. Your prototypes of a class as a classroom is what enabled you to easily recognize a picture of classrooms from 100 and 4,000 years ago.

We want to call attention to another prominent characteristic in the Ohio model school image. The teachers and students look alike. They look as if they all were from the same homogeneous group, like members of what is often called a "traditional" family. The students are also doing the same type of activity. This multileveled homogeneity is common in many schools and school images. In other words, the predominant prototype of a classroom or schooling almost always includes homogeneity.

We want to probe this last characteristic a bit more, because our classroom prototype is also based on a fundamental metaphor: NATIONS and SCHOOLS are FAMILIES. Research by George Lakoff (1987, 2002, 2006b, 2008), for example, shows that we use phrases such as "father of our country" and "sons and daughters going off to war" because we think of our nation as a larger version of our own family. The same is true for schools: We think of and promote schools as teams and families, with teachers acting as surrogate parents to their students (see, e.g., Baker, 1991; Cranston, 2010; Demir, 2007; Wincek, 1995).

However, as Lakoff (2002) has described, and as many of us have likely experienced, there are two basic FAMILY prototypes for the NATIONS and SCHOOLS are FAMILIES metaphor. One FAMILY prototype is derived from the "strict authority-based" family, and the second is organized around the "caring nurturance–based" family. Further, we find that these family prototypes parallel two metaphors for understanding how people learn and should teach: the predominant CONDUIT and EMPTY VESSEL metaphors and the secondary GROWTH metaphor. We will describe these two education models, including the linked groups of metaphors and prototypes in turn, starting with the currently predominant one built on the CONDUIT and EMPTY VESSEL metaphors for learning and teaching. After we describe each education model, we will explain why we believe that the one based on the CONDUIT and EMPTY VESSEL metaphors is the predominant model underlying our current educationalese.

The EMPTY VESSEL and CONDUIT Metaphors for Teaching and Learning

The predominant mental model for learning and teaching has many labels, including "factory," "transmission," "traditional," "mechanic," "authoritarian," and "banking." All these labels refer to a model composed of two sets of primary metaphors: the CONDUIT metaphor for communication and the EMPTY VESSEL metaphor for the brain or mind.

The CONDUIT metaphor for communication was most likely first named and described by Michael Reddy in 1979, and developed in detail by George Lakoff and Mark Johnson in their books *Metaphors We Live By* (2003) and *Philosophy in the Flesh* (1999). It has been applied to teaching and learning by many people, including the authors (see, e.g., Haas, 2007a, 2007b, 2008; Haas & Fischman, 2010). Possibly the most notable description of this type of schooling is Freire's criticism of the banking model of education in *Pedagogy of the Oppressed* (1970/1993), though his book precedes the work of Reddy and of Lakoff and Johnson, and does not name the CONDUIT metaphor explicitly.

Lakoff and Johnson (2003) describe the elemental metaphors that together make up the CONDUIT metaphor of communication this way:

> IDEAS or MEANINGS are OBJECTS
> LINGUISTIC EXPRESSIONS (such as words) are CONTAINERS
> COMMUNICATION is SENDING.

Lakoff and Johnson (2003) explain the process this way: "the speaker puts ideas (objects) into words (containers) and sends them (along a conduit) to a hearer who takes this idea/objects out of the words/containers" (p. 10). Applied to education, an additional elemental metaphor is added to the list: The BRAIN (or mind) is an EMPTY VESSEL.

Freire (1970/1993) does a good job of describing how the CONDUIT metaphor, with the addition of the BRAIN is an EMPTY VESSEL metaphor, have impacted education: In his critique of "transmission" teaching, he describes how students are treated as "receptacles" that are to be "filled" with the "content of the teacher's narration" (p. 1).

The strict authority-based prototype of the NATIONS and SCHOOLS are FAMILIES metaphor is the moral foundation of the CONDUIT and the MIND is an EMPTY VESSEL metaphors of learning and teaching. The "strict authority-based" prototype informing the NATION is a FAMILY metaphor is built on the idea that there are timeless, universal (capital T) Truths that are handed down from the nation's leaders to families through the father, on down through the mother, and then to the children (Lakoff, 2002). The first obligation is to learn and follow these Truths through obedience to the authorities. Individuals who follow these rules will prosper.

In schools, these Truths are delivered through prescribed curricula, approved textbooks, and standardized tests using a top-down system enforced by principals through teachers, and down to students. Teachers should deliver the unquestionable curricula to students, who should accept it by memorizing and practicing what their teachers give them until they can repeat it accurately. Successful students strictly follow school rules as the way to learn these Truths.

For the logic of the CONDUIT and EMPTY VESSEL metaphors to have an internal logic for education—that is, to provide a workable way to understand and implement schooling—two key elements of teaching and learning have to be understood in specific ways. First, facts, ideas, concepts, and meanings—essentially, right answers—must be concrete, timeless, and universal. As a result, what a teacher says and what each and every student in class hears and understands are the same. Second, right answers are directly stored in free spaces in your brain (or mind). In other words, learning is filling the empty spaces in your brain with more and more information.

We imagine and hope that many readers will disagree at some level with what we just wrote. That is good, because both of these key element understandings are wrong, as we will explain in detail in Chapter 3. Nevertheless, we contend that the CONDUIT and EMPTY VESSEL metaphors are the predominant way most people understand learning and teaching, at least initially at the fast-thinking level. Here are some examples of how and why we experience them all around us.

The CONDUIT and EMPTY VESSEL metaphors make sense because it feels like we understand and learn things directly from the world. A friend says something and we understand it instantly. We look at a picture or read words and we "get" what they are about without a pause. It feels, at least to our conscious minds, that what we sense about the world involves information going straight into our brains. As we will explain in Chapter 3, this is not what happens in our brains, but it often intuitively feels that way to us.

We also use the CONDUIT and EMPTY VESSEL metaphors in our everyday speech. We say things like:

"Michaela gave me the right answer."
"Leslie's writing is filled with meaning."
"Put that idea in the back of your mind."
"Jessica had a hard time putting her idea into words."
"I can't seem to get your idea out of my head."

We communicate all the time using these metaphors, which strengthens their dominance in our understanding, including in the wiring of the synapses in our brains (Feldman, 2008). As we described earlier, most of us have also experienced countless hours of the school practices that result from these metaphors. It is hard to count the amount of time we spent in school reading, memorizing, and repeating right answers that were "transmitted" to us from teacher lectures, videos, and textbooks (Haas & Poynor, 2005). For example, well-known author, English professor, and education policy commentator E. D. Hirsch, in his book *Cultural Literacy* (1987), followed by his *Core Knowledge Sequence*,[1] and much later in his *The Making of Americans* (2009), advocates that this is what education should be about: Schools need to deliver key facts about U.S. and Western culture that students memorize to create a common understanding of what American society is about. As we will describe in Chapter 3, forced memorization of facts where students see little connection to their daily lives or have little opportunity to practice the skills needed to apply what they learn to real, authentic activities will not bring about the communal understandings that Hirsch desires beyond, possibly, how boring social studies can be.

Before we describe some of the practices that come from the logic of this factory model of education, we want to describe further its dominance, including the dominance of the CONDUIT and EMPTY VESSEL metaphors and the strict authority-based prototype in our educationalese. Not only have most of our education experiences been versions of factory model education, the factory model is also continually reinforced as natural and good in the media. Let's examine how some popular movies have portrayed teaching, learning, and diversity.

To start, think about the movie *Dead Poets Society* (1989) and an exchange between Robin Williams's character, the new high school teacher John Keating, and the headmaster Galen Nolan (played by Norman Lloyd), when discussing the point of their prep school education:

Keating: I always thought the idea of education was to learn to think for yourself.
Nolan: At these boys' age? Not on your life!

The John Keating character does not follow this advice. Instead, he forces the students out of their rowed seats and the automatic parroting of the texts that they were assigned. This results in a student suicide and Keating being fired in disgrace.

Or, think about Michelle Pfeiffer's character, ex–U.S. marine turned high school teacher, LouAnne Johnson, in *Dangerous Minds* (1995). Michelle Pfeiffer was White and basically middle-class, while her students were mostly African American or Latino and poor. To motivate the students, the LouAnne Johnson character dresses in jeans and a leather jacket, teaches them some karate, uses popular music in place of some of the classic poetry, and takes the students to a theme park as a reward for their hard work. In the end, one of her students is killed and she decides not to return for a second year.

Contrast these movies with the film *Stand and Deliver* (1988). In *Stand and Deliver*, the hero is a character based on the real life of Jaime Escalante (played by Edward James Olmos), who left his computer job for the Burroughs Corporation to teach high school computer science, but ends up becoming a star math teacher. In the movie, Escalante comes to a poor, dysfunctional, and dangerous East Los Angeles high school to teach computer science, but decides instead to teach calculus. Jaime Escalante is Latino and most of his students are Latino and of other minority ethnic backgrounds. In his first 2 years of teaching at this school, he gets his currently lowperforming students to excel by pushing them longer and harder to move from struggling with fractions to solving calculus problems in record time. The students remain in rows and do worksheet after worksheet, practice test after practice test, until they are able to do the same types of problems on the Advanced Placement Calculus test. In the movie, nearly every one of the approximately 25 students who starts the class takes and passes the AP Calculus test—twice.

In sum, whether school is the central subject of a movie or television show or just one of the many contexts, the vast majority of the representations are similar: Homogeneous student bodies and faculty, the delivery of information from teacher to students, and students expected to practice memorizing and repeating what the teacher presented are what school is, while deviations from that representation end in disaster or simply are not represented at all.

We do not mean to say that contrary representations never happen. There are a few other school-based movies and televisions shows with different results—*To Sir with Love* (1967), starring Sidney Poitier, and *Glee* (2009–present) are two examples. The key point is not that school-based movies and television shows never present other concepts of teaching and learning besides those based on the CONDUIT and EMPTY VESSEL metaphors and the strict authority-based prototype of homogeneous, fact-delivery schools (though we would argue that the vast majority do not), but rather how readily we accept these premises as logical and normal. From what we see in the movies and on television, it seems like we don't need "fancy" teaching activities; we just need tough teachers who know the material and can control a class and students who will work hard doing lots and lots of decontextualized problems. That seems like common sense when thinking with the CONDUIT and EMPTY VESSEL metaphors and strict authority-based prototype of learning and teaching.

But, is this portrayal of teaching and learning accurate? Does this simple success formula work? The answer is no on both counts, which is why what *Stand and Deliver* portrays as the commonsense logic that an isolated teacher and class working hard for several months can achieve phenomenal results is also an example of *rightly wrong* thinking. Let's go behind the movie *Stand and Deliver* and look at the real story (Jesness, 2002). In real life, the students who struggled with fractions in Jaime Escalante's first math class at Garfield High School were not the same students who became the first of his students to pass the AP Calculus test. Jaime Escalante did not teach calculus until his 5th year at Garfield High School. Fourteen students started in his first calculus class, five continued until the end of the year, and two of those five passed the AP Calculus exam.[2] Further, the real-life success of Jaime Escalante happened because he and many other teachers developed a system where they worked with students over many years, which enabled the students to be able to be successful at calculus near the end of high school. Jerry Jesness (2002), who wrote an investigative article on Jaime Escalante's work, concluded that the unrealistic *Stand and Deliver* message of a lone teacher pushing his students to achieve phenomenal results in a short amount of time actually hinders truly effective reform measures—the creation of a system of teacher and student supports that took a team of educators a decade to develop.

> The *Stand and Deliver* message, that the touch of a master could bring unmotivated students from arithmetic to calculus in a single year, was preached in schools throughout the nation. While the film did a great service to education by showing what students from disadvantaged backgrounds can achieve in demanding classes, the Hollywood fiction had at least one negative side effect. By showing students moving from fractions to calculus in a single year, it gave the false impression that students can neglect their studies for several years and then be redeemed by a few months of hard work.
>
> This Hollywood message had a pernicious effect on teacher training. The lessons of Escalante's patience and hard work in building his program, especially his attention to the classes that fed into calculus, were largely ignored in the faculty workshops and college education classes that routinely showed *Stand and Deliver* to their students. To the pedagogues, how Escalante

succeeded mattered less than the mere fact that he succeeded. They were happy to cheer Escalante the icon; they were less interested in learning from Escalante the teacher. They were like physicians getting excited about a colleague who can cure cancer without wanting to know how to replicate the cure. (p. 1)

We hear lots of praise of the virtues of fast thinking common sense. We also cautiously like our fast-thinking reactions and understand that it is a part of our thinking and decisionmaking processes that can be beneficial in our daily lives and is necessary for achieving expertise, when it is accurate (more on this in Chapter 4). But in this case, the CONDUIT and EMPTY VESSEL metaphors of learning and teaching that make the movie *Stand and Deliver* feel "right" are not what happened in real life and thus they result in *rightly wrong* thinking about education. A key element of embodied cognition is that repeated experiences with something builds a dominant fast-thinking model of that something as natural and good—as common sense—regardless of whether it is accurate or correct (Lakoff & Johnson, 1999, 2003). So, how common are the CONDUIT and EMPTY VESSEL metaphors of learning and the strict authority-based prototype versions of teaching and schooling? As we described above, they are all very common in the media. What we have observed in numerous schools, and what we have heard from thousands of teachers and administrators over the years, is that teaching and schooling based on these metaphors and prototypes are also common in everyday life. That is why every person we have asked to draw math classes drew factory model–like classrooms and why it is so easy to recognize the two photographs (shown earlier in the chapter) as classrooms—this is how we and everyone we know experiences schooling both directly and through the media. Thus, as a result of our school and media experiences, our language, and the feeling that information goes directly into our brains, the predominant way we understand learning—at least initially at the fast-thinking level—is that people pile up "right answers" in their heads like they might fill a bucket with sand.

Because of the predominance of CONDUIT and EMPTY VESSEL metaphors and their associated education models in our educationalese, we want to do some more unpacking of the key elements. First, what does a good teacher look like and how should he or she act? What does good teaching look like? Because learning is understood as filling an empty mind with more information, then good teaching is delivering as much information as possible to students. How do we efficiently deliver the most information to the most students? Teachers lecture, telling students *the right answers* to remember or giving them an algorithm, like the butterfly common denominator for adding and subtracting fractions, in math.[3] Students read textbooks, visit websites, or watch videos full of *the right answers*. Students then practice repeating *the right answers* for homework and then repeat them again on the test. The CONDUIT and EMPTY VESSEL metaphors result in a model of education that focuses on transmitting as much information as possible for students to store in their minds for use at some, as yet undetermined, point in the future. We look to improve education by simplifying all the knowledge and activities that students do and delivering them to students in prepackaged, ready-to-digest form with the belief that this simplification "pre-work" will enable them to learn more and do so faster. A good teacher thus has a quiet, orderly classroom, such as with students sitting in rows of individual desks, so she can deliver discrete bits of information to the students. Students then memorize and practice lots of examples of this delivered information, moving on to the next bit of material when most of the class can repeat the current material on a test or homework assignment.

With the CONDUIT and EMPTY VESSEL metaphors in mind, teachers must first and foremost know their subject-matter content. They cannot deliver what they do not already possess. Next, they must be good disciplinarians so they can maintain order in the classroom, to ensure that information can be delivered. Teachers do not have to understand much about the learning process because the process is understood simply as students storing information in their heads. In this way, the entire teaching process is constrained to a simplistic notion of knowledge transfer that ignores massive bodies of research on effective pedagogy (see, e.g., Gee, 2007; Darling-Hammond, 1997, 2010).

Second, what does a student look like and how should they act? Good students sit at their desks and do their exercises. They ask questions when they do not understand how to do something they are told to do, but they do not question why they are doing what they are doing or what the right answer is. Students, as viewed through the CONDUIT and EMPTY VESSEL metaphors, are consciously rational learners. This means that what the teacher says and means is exactly what the students hear and understand. Students are understood to be blank slates when it comes to most topics: They do not interpret facts that they hear in school through different experiences (or lenses) because most, if not all, information is concrete, objective, and universal, and thus can be delivered in the form of right answers. Again, information is understood as discrete factoids delivered as right answers from teacher to student through mutually understood words.

Next, if you use the EMPTY VESSEL and CONDUIT metaphors to create schools, you end up with a school system that focuses on transmitting as many right answers as possible.[4] Many readers might applaud this education goal; however, as we will explain in Chapter 4, right answer transmission will rarely, if ever, result in expert or even usable knowledge by itself. Here is a quote from OECD that describes U.S. math students' ability, as a partial explanation of low U.S. scores compared with the scores of other industrialized nations on the international PISA test:

> Students in the United States have particular weaknesses in performing mathematics tasks with higher cognitive demands, such as taking real-world situations, translating them into mathematical terms, and interpreting mathematical aspects in real-world problems. (OECD, 2013a, p. 1)

This general deficit in the math ability of U.S. students, we contend, results from an overemphasis in schools on the delivery of right answers and not enough time spent on actually solving real, authentic problems with math (see e.g., Darling-Hammond, 1997, 2010).

Here, we describe key details for how an education system should operate based on the logic of the factory model of education built on the CONDUIT and EMPTY VESSEL metaphors of teaching and learning. It should appear familiar, if not comfortable, to nearly everyone. If one sees ideas and facts as discrete objects that can be poured into the empty minds of rational students, then lecturing and reading information from textbooks or an iPad or watching videos must be the most effective and efficient methods of teaching. Lots of information can be delivered as right answers from teacher to the students, who learn by storing that information directly in their heads. Further, if students are not learning something, then lessons should be broken down into smaller pieces and spoon-fed to the students. Here, the metaphor changes slightly to ideas as food objects, which students consume, but the concept of delivery and direct absorption remains the same. If students still are not learning according to the test, then they must not be trying or they must be resisting because all they have to do to learn is take in the information the teacher has delivered, especially when other students are learning the same information in the same way. If others can do it, then so can they, if they put forth enough effort. Remember, in this (mis)understanding of learning, everyone is essentially doing the same thing: taking timeless, objective information and storing it directly into their heads. Because all the students received the same right answers from the teacher's lecture to the whole class or from the textbook, iPad, or video, and because they are storing those *right answers* into the empty spaces in their brains, then those who did not learn *the right answers* either did not try or must have a learning disability.

Similar logic applies to the teachers of these students—the teachers of underachieving students must not know *the right answers* well enough, must not be trying hard enough, or must not be doing what they are supposed to be doing to deliver the same *right answers* that other teachers of other students have successfully been able to deliver. Basically, this comes down to issues of classroom management, with perhaps some additional emphasis on knowing the content. If you can control the class well enough to deliver the required *right answers*, then you have taught. Punishment, often phrased as the only true form of "accountability" for both students and teachers, then becomes the preferred method of motivating improvements in learning and teaching.

Given an understanding that knowledge comes in the form of discrete objects and that all student brains are full of empty spaces for inserting *the right answers*, then schools can be run like production facilities. In other words, schools should be run like businesses, or better yet, like factories. Following this logic further, teaching, or delivering the knowledge objects to students, can be made more efficient through "mechanized" or prepackaged programs of one-size-fits-all scripted units that dictate every action by both teachers and students. These are sometimes called "teacher-proof" lessons because no teaching skills (or thinking) are needed. All the teacher needs to do is deliver the lesson and *the right answers* and control the class so the students can focus enough to store *the right answers* in the empty spaces in their brains. In this factory model of schools, students then become the product output of schools. We create standards and curricula for what students should learn in each subject, the teacher delivers the predetermined *right answers*, and then we measure the quality of schools by the standardized test scores of students. Reform, then, means implementing the programs and practices that other successful schools (those with high test scores) have done successfully in other places with other students. Again, the idea is that if others can do it, then so can you, with enough effort.

As we stated at the beginning of the chapter, the strict authority-based prototype of the SCHOOL is a FAMILY metaphor provides additional moral and logical support to the CONDUIT and EMPTY VESSEL metaphors and the resulting model of education focused on transmitting as much information as efficiently as possible. The strict authority-based prototype provides logical and moral support for the timeless, universal nature of Truth and the imperative of *right answer* transmission.

Another metaphor, the FREEDOM is LACK OF CONSTRAINT metaphor, also provides logical and even moral support for aspects of education and related social practices (Lakoff, 2007). FREEDOM is LACK OF CONSTRAINT is the predominant of two key metaphoric understandings of freedom. The other is FREEDOM is SUPPORT. This latter metaphoric understanding of freedom is not as strongly embedded in U.S. thinking as the FREEDOM is LACK OF CONSTRAINT metaphor, in part because the physical experience of FREEDOM is LACK OF CONSTRAINT is generally more obvious and direct than the FREEDOM is SUPPORT experience (Lakoff, 2007). We all have direct experiences feeling the physical freedom of not being restrained and this makes it easy to link that physical experience to nonphysical ideas. For example, the FREEDOM is LACK OF CONSTRAINT metaphor can be used to justify the denial of public social services to support student learning by freeing us from the restraints of government bureaucracy. Don't mandate teacher certification, free lunch programs, living wages, or universal health care—just get the bureaucracy out of the way so good teachers can teach and smart students can succeed. The notion that good teachers and smart students are not "made"—in the sense that they require time, practice, study and reflection to develop—but born, and that students need supports to enable their learning do not enter the discussion because they do not seem necessary when fast and slow thinking are based on the factory model of education, supported by the FREEDOM is LACK OF CONSTRAINT metaphor.

Before we describe how people learn and the more accurate GROWTH metaphor for learning and teaching, we want to show in the next chapter another example of how our current CONDUIT and EMPTY VESSEL–based educationalese impacts the education policies and practices that we promote. In the Introduction, we described how the Common Core State Standards are being promoted despite there being no direct evidence of the Common Core (or any standards by themselves) improving student achievement, while National Board Certification for teachers is being ignored even though it consistently does have such supporting evidence. After describing the logic of the CONDUIT and EMPTY VESSEL–based educationalese, it seems straightforward to explain the difference in popularity. It is much more important to student achievement to state explicitly the right answers that should be delivered by teachers to students in the form of the Common Core State Standards than it is to extensively train teachers on child development, effective pedagogy, and content knowledge so they can understand each child's learning needs and develop appropriate learning opportunities. The "need" for the Common Core State Standards rather than an expansion of National Board Certification perhaps seems so obvious at the fast-thinking level that slow-thinking deliberations are either not necessary or are trumped by our fast-thinking reactions. It is an example of this latter trumping of evidence by our fast-thinking reactions that we will explore in the next chapter.

CHAPTER 2

Can Educationalese Trump Contrary Evidence and Attempts at Contrary Logic?

Our initial fast-thinking reaction to an education idea—whether we think it is smart or dumb—has a strong impact on our slow thinking about that idea as well. One fast-thinking influence is known as Confirmation Bias (Kahneman, 2011). Confirmation Bias is the tendency to unconsciously see and absorb information that adheres to our current view. If we currently believe that charter schools, for example, are the solution to our education problems, then positive reports about charter schools are more likely to catch our eye and to seem rigorous and logical than negative reports about charter schools (see, e.g., Bartels, 2002). To a certain degree, this is what we see in the support of Morgan Polikoff (2014) for the Common Core State Standards that we described in the Introduction. He found some studies that supported standards *along with other factors* such as accountability threats that changed teacher behaviors in some ways that led to student achievement improvements and concluded that standards alone will improve student achievement. At the same time, Polikoff (2014) did not discuss at all the direct contrary evidence from Bracey (2009) and Whitehurst (2009) that there is no one-to-one relationship between standards and student achievement. Although an argument can be made for the need for the Common Core State Standards as part of a set of education reforms (see Whitehurst, 2009, and also our discussion in Chapter 5), there is no evidence—at least none that we are aware of—that standards alone or that standards as the primary focus of education reform will improve student achievement.

Perhaps not discussing the work of Bracey (2009) and Whitehurst (2009) was Polikoff's oversight. It is certainly very difficult to know about all the research in any area of education, and we certainly will not require that—even of an education professor. At the same time, we must be very aware of our tendencies to see what we already believe to be true according to our initial fast-thinking reaction—Confirmation Bias—as well as the flip side, ignoring or rejecting evidence that is contrary to our current views. According to Arbesman (2012) and Churchland (2013), the Semmelweis effect, or the trumping of consciously examined facts by the automatic response of our unconscious mind, is quite common. In the mid-1800s, Hungarian physician Ignaz Semmelweis demonstrated that washing hands with chlorinated lime would disinfect them and reduce death by infection in patients. He demonstrated this positive effect by showing that when hand-washing was done before examining women in the obstetrics ward, the women's mortality rates from infection decreased from about 35% down to 1%, especially when a doctor washed his hands between dissecting cadavers and examining his female patients. Unfortunately, Semmelweis's evidence was dismissed as absurd and even offensive by leading doctors of the day. He could not persuade many of his colleagues to even test his handwashing idea. As a result, handwashing by doctors did not become common practice until many years after Semmelweis's death. Research in psychology has consistently shown that once we have a strong belief that something is true, we will often consciously dismiss contrary evidence in order to justify our belief (Haidt, 2012) and that when we are confronted by evidence that our position is wrong or illogical, we may become more resistant to changing our mind, rather than more reflective and open, especially when the issue is very important to us (see, e.g., Ginges, Atran, Medin, & Shikaki, 2007).

We believe that the current educationalese based on the CONDUIT and EMPTY VESSEL metaphors for learning and teaching and the prototypes of homogeneous students and class activities have created tendencies for people to support programs and practices that fit with this factory model of education, despite consistent evidence that it does not work. In other words, the current educationalese has led to *rightly wrong* thinking about the effectiveness of the factory model of education: It seems so internally logical according to the CONDUIT and EMPTY VESSEL metaphors and the homogeneous prototypes of schooling of our fast thinking that we are more comfortable consciously rejecting contrary evidence in our slow thinking than we are using the contrary evidence to better our understanding of what works to improve student achievement at both the fast- and slow-thinking levels. We will examine the work of Michelle Rhee and her StudentsFirst organization as an example of the power of this *rightly wrong* thinking.

Michelle Rhee's education advocacy organization, StudentsFirst, released its second annual State Policy Report Card in January 2014. The report card issues grades from A to F and ranks states on the quality of their state education policies, which it determines by "how well its laws and policies align with StudentsFirst's Policy Agenda" (StudentsFirst, 2014, p. 5).

StudentsFirst created 24 policies of interest, of which 12 are anchor policies that receive more weight in the Policy Report Card. The 12 anchor policies include the following high-score criteria:

- Teacher and principal evaluations of which at least 50% is based on meeting specific student growth targets
- That evaluations are not subject to collective bargaining agreements
- That states allow alternative certification for all grades and subjects and the demonstration of "subject-matter/content knowledge in the area(s) taught through a content exam" (p. 57), but does not require any knowledge of child development or pedagogy
- Merit pay
- Annual school report cards based on student achievement scores and parent triggers to take over what are determined to be low-performing schools
- Student vouchers and supports for charter school expansion
- Direct state and/or mayoral control of what are determined to be low-performing public schools
- No class size limits on grades 4 and above
- Replacement of educator pension plans with "portable retirement benefits" (p. 64)

The StudentsFirst policy agenda fits perfectly with the factory model of schooling and its underlying CONDUIT, EMPTY VESSEL, and FREEDOM is LACK OF CONSTRAINT metaphors. For example, the proposals for alternative certification, removing evaluations from collective bargaining agreements, increasing vouchers and charter schools, and replacing pensions with "portable retirement benefits" are all forms of removing restraints from the education system. Further, the emphasis on content knowledge over pedagogical and child development knowledge and the proposal to remove class size limits makes sense if teaching and learning are merely the delivery and direct storage of timeless, universal, capital-T Truths. In Chapter 5, we will discuss the current state of research evidence linking these reforms with improvements in student achievement. But for now, let's make an easier comparison. How do the StudentsFirst state policy rankings compare with the readily available results from the National Assessment of Educational Progress (NAEP) (National Center for Education Statistics [NCES], 2013b)? And, further, how did StudentsFirst react to the comparison?

Rather badly, on both counts. It turns out that the 2014 StudentsFirst Policy Report grades are in strong disagreement with the most recent NAEP test scores (NCES, 2013b). For example, the top five StudentsFirst Policy Report Card (2014) states—Louisiana, Florida, Indiana, Rhode Island, and

Washington, DC—had some of the lowest NAEP test scores in reading and math. Eighth-grade students in Louisiana, the top-ranked StudentsFirst policy state, ranked 49th out of 52 (the 50 states, plus Washington, DC, and Department of Defense schools) in reading and 47th in math on the NAEP. Washington, DC ranked fifth on the StudentsFirst Policy Report Card, while its 8th-grade students ranked 52nd out of 52 on the NAEP in both reading and math. In contrast, StudentsFirst gave low policy rankings to states whose 8th-grade students ranked high on the NAEP. For example, Massachusetts' 8th-graders were ranked #1 in reading and math on the NAEP, but StudentsFirst ranked Massachusetts at #21 in state policy reforms. Similarly, Connecticut and New Jersey 8th-graders ranked #2 and #3 in NAEP reading scores, but their states were ranked #24 and #31, respectively, on the 2014 StudentsFirst Policy Report Card.

The NAEP results make the 2014 StudentsFirst state Policy Report Card seem rather ludicrous. If the StudentsFirst policy agenda and its 2014 state Policy Report Card were effective in enabling high student achievement, then we would expect there to be at least a medium to possibly strong association between the most recent NAEP rankings and the StudentsFirst 2014 state Policy Report Card rankings. If the StudentsFirst policy agenda ideas, such as charter schools, alternative teacher certification, unlimited class sizes in grade 4 and above, and the replacement of teacher pensions with smaller 401k-type plans, were making positive impacts on student achievement, then the states that have implemented more of these ideas and that have higher StudentsFirst rankings would also have higher NAEP test score averages across their students, compared with those states that have implemented fewer of StudentsFirst's education ideas. But this wasn't the result. In general, the opposite occurred. The association between NAEP test scores and StudentsFirst policy rankings is very weak, as the rankings were often opposite, as we described above. (On the other hand, if there is really no empirical evidence to support a claim that state policies can impact student achievement, then a state Policy Report Card becomes, in effect, a meaningless wish list.)

StudentsFirst should have known about this negative relationship between its 2014 Policy Report Card results and the most recent NAEP scores. Why? Because StudentsFirst used nearly the exact same methodology for its first Policy Report Card in 2013, and it received this exact critique from several major news outlets, including *Daily Kos* (Clawson, 2013) and the *Washington Post* (Strauss, 2013). Certainly, StudentsFirst, a national, multi-million-dollar organization (Resmovits, 2012), must have been aware of the discrepancy between its 2013 state policy rankings and the NAEP scores of the students in those states. Yet, it published a second report in January 2014 with the same policy agenda, nearly identical grading policy criteria, and very similar state rankings. Clearly, readily available contrary evidence has had little impact on StudentsFirst's steadfast belief that its policy agenda must be effective in improving student achievement. This, to us, is another example of the power of fast thinking on education ideas, and how even inaccurate fast thinking can stop what should have been corrective slow thinking. In this case, it appears that StudentsFirst has let the current factory model educationalese trump some strong NAEP evidence that the policies that StudentsFirst advocates (including alternative certification, student test score–based teacher evaluations, vouchers and charter schools, large class sizes, and the replacement of teacher pension plans with 401K-type savings programs) will not improve student achievement.

We understand that there may be more to the StudentsFirst education agenda than the Semmelweis Reflex and well-intentioned but *rightly wrong* thinking. People can also promote their own economic, political, and ideological interests ahead of evidence-based education reforms. However, these are not the stated reasons for the policies, programs, and practices people support. Rather, proponents of an education reform will justify their support with the logic of their fast-thinking models and the level of evidence they feel is needed to be convincing. The more the logic fits the current educationalese, the less actual supporting evidence is likely to be needed. At the same time, Confirmation Bias and the Semmelweis Reflex demonstrate that contrary evidence alone will rarely convince people to change their initial reactions about an education reform. To promote evidence-based education reforms, we must know the evidence both for and against current education reforms, and we must also know and be able to articulate the accurate metaphors and prototypes that are the foundation of the logic of evidence-based reforms as well as the inaccurate ones that support *rightly wrong* thinking. In other words, to promote evidence-based reform, we must develop and align our fast and slow thinking with accurate fast-thinking models and plenty of slow-thinking evidence. This is especially difficult to do when the current educationalese is *rightly wrong* thinking, such as the factory model of education based on the CONDUIT and EMPTY VESSEL metaphors and the homogeneous schooling prototypes we have described.

In the next two chapters, we will describe in detail how people learn, how the way people learn is different from what seems logical according to the CONDUIT and EMPTY VESSEL metaphors, and how a GROWTH metaphor for learning and teaching is more accurate and therefore can support better education decisions at both fast- and slow-thinking levels.

CHAPTER 3

Fast and Slow Rationality and Learning

There are many aspects to learning, more than can be described in full detail in this book.[1] We will focus here on two foundational aspects for which there is general consensus that students should learn in school: (1) conceptual understandings of key ideas across the various academic disciplines and (2) developing more expert knowledge about how to apply those conceptual understandings in real-world situations. We will explain below how people learn conceptual understandings and how we develop and align our fast and slow thinking to become experts in a specific activity or discipline. As you should see by the end of this chapter, how we learn and become more expert does not fit well with the CONDUIT, EMPTY VESSEL, and FREEDOM IS LACK OF CONSTRAINT metaphors. In Chapter 4, we will describe the LEARNING IS GROWTH metaphor as a more accurate way of understanding learning and teaching and thus a better way to develop and align our fast and slow thinking when we are trying to decide which proposed education reforms will likely be effective in improving student achievement.

Conceptual Understandings

As we have already started discussing in the first three chapters, people learn by constructing concepts and models of the world through the use of metaphors and prototypes. We do that by comparing new things that we experience with what we currently understand about those things, and we do this mental construction mostly unconsciously but also consciously. We want to begin this chapter with some example activities to help show how this process happens. The activities are short, taking about a minute or so each to do, and they are very powerful because it is hard to ignore them. Their implications may make you uncomfortable, and you may want to argue with them. This is a common reaction and is important to recognize before you start.

Here is the first example activity.

Think about all the misunderstandings that go on during the conversations we have every single day. Someone says one thing, but we hear something else. It's just like in the telephone game we played as children: We hear some words that are said quickly, which creates some ambiguity, and because we don't know the intended context, we can "hear" lots of different words depending on whatever context we imagine is intended. At the end of the game, everyone laughs when we hear what was originally said and how different it is from the final message at the end of the line of people.

Although there are lots of possible words that we can hear during the telephone game, the possibilities are not unlimited. They are bounded by what we believe is common sense regarding which words would go together to make a reasonable, logical phrase—in other words, our prototype of what a phrase, said in English, should be. What we consider a logical, commonsense phrase in English comes from the understandings that we are constantly constructing through reading, writing, listening and speaking all day long for years and years.

This is the key point about learning: We construct what we know. This idea is so central to teaching and learning—and the human experience in general—that it is worth presenting several arguments to make sure we drive the point home.

An important point we want to highlight is that we understand and use the notion of *construction* a bit differently from the common use of the word. Most people identify construction with a systematic and conscious effort that involves assembling discrete parts into a predetermined structure, similar to the idea of constructing a building with LEGOs or constructing a house with wood and nails. Our use of the word *construction* refers to the automatic, unstoppable pattern-making ability of our brains. We cannot stop our brains from constructing understandings because such processes are automatic and unconscious. We can override some of them with conscious thoughts, practice, and reflection, but we cannot completely stop the initial, automatic, unconscious construction that occurs. Here are three examples to see for yourself how this notion of construction works. Look at the scrambled word example below.

Can yuo raed tihs? Are yuo srpruesid? You can aulaclty uesdnatnrd waht you are rdanieg. In fcat, if yuo are fulnet in Egnislh you cnnaot not raed tihs. Yuor bairn rdaes this atoullimatacy and yuo conant sotp ylsouerf. Amzanig, huh?

What do you notice? That you could read the example—automatically. Without being told the pattern and even before you could consciously articulate it, you figured it out and read the passage. In fact, you cannot stop yourself from reading it. If we gave you more scrambled words like these in logical sentences, you would automatically understand what the correct words were. Just for fun, here's another, similar example, except in this one there are missing letters, not scrambled ones.

Yo ca re d t is jus fin , eve with t e miss g l tt rs.

These puzzles are analogous to the process of knowledge construction in general. Our brain is a meaning-maker that uses pattern construction, and it builds on what we already know, independently of the accuracy of what we know. This automatic, unconscious "constructing" is how we create the categories and prototypes introduced above. We automatically and unconsciously try to fit new information into the patterns we already have in our mind in order to make sense of them. If they fit, then our patterns are reinforced. If they do not fit, then some combination of two processes happens unconsciously and automatically: We force the new information to fit into our existing understandings by ignoring some or all of the characteristics of the new information, or we reconstruct our current understandings based on this new information. The key aspect to remember here is that there is no objectively accurate or inaccurate process for constructing meanings—the accuracy and pertinence of the understandings that we construct are established through what works in our particular lived experiences, which are historical and social in nature.

The telephone game and the scrambled word puzzles above are examples of our first response to new information: We took new, ambiguous information and fit it into patterns we already had about the English language. With the scrambled words, there was a clear correct pattern, our brains figured it out unconsciously, and we read the words, so we also consciously knew that we got the right answer. In the telephone game, there was no obvious one correct answer, but there were obvious wrong answers—when the words we thought we heard did not form a logical phrase, then we knew that what we constructed from what we heard was not right. Nevertheless, we constructed something as best we could, based on what we already knew.

Optical illusions, like the ones shown in Figures 3.1 and 3.2, also demonstrate the automatic, unstoppable pattern-making ability of our brains. In Figure 3.1, we focus on the parts of the picture that enable us to see a pattern that looks like something logical—here, either the vase or the two faces—and we ignore the other parts of the picture that keep us from seeing it. We each tend to see one or the other initially, but we can also tell ourselves to see the other, and we can experience the picture changing so that one or the other dominates. We can inject some conscious thought to focus or override aspects of our unconscious thinking.

Figure 3.1. Rubin's Vase Optical Illusion

It is important to remember that there are no objectively right patterns that are being constructed. For example, look at the optical illusion in Figure 3.2. What do you notice?

Figure 3.2. Elephant Optical Illusion

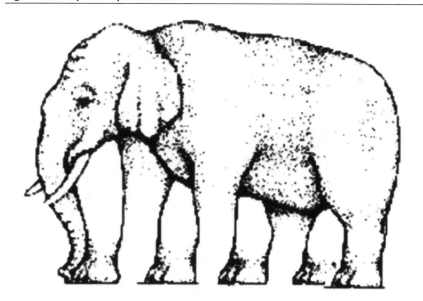

Our brains continually try to construct a fifth leg for the elephant because the lines provide enough information on a fifth leg that it prompts us to use our current knowledge of elephant legs to complete the pattern and form the fifth leg. We consciously know that elephants only have four legs, but in this case our unconscious mind still tries to form a fifth leg because there is enough evidence in the picture to prompt it to do so. Sometimes our conscious and unconscious minds don't agree.

Here is one final example. Look at these connected lines.

H

By themselves, these lines do not seem to represent anything we know. But with some context, our brains can complete a known pattern.

CAT

Now, the connected lines seem to be an *A*, which forms the word *CAT*.

But it doesn't have to be *A*. With different context clues, your brain will automatically form a new pattern.

THE

Here, your brain identifies *H* to form *THE*. Different context clues mean a different pattern.

Again, the pattern-making process happens unconsciously and automatically, and we cannot really control it. We can sometimes consciously override the initial reaction, but we cannot make it go away. We see this in two-part optical illusions, such as the faces and vase picture. We can sometimes make ourselves see one or the other image. But it takes effort, and sometimes what we see switches back on our conscious mind.

We want to repeat this key point again: We construct understandings. Understandings are not discrete, concrete things, and they cannot be delivered in complete form from one person (textbook, video, teacher) to another. Understandings derive from the automatic, unstoppable pattern-making ability of our brains. We take what we gather from our senses and interpret it through our experiences and understandings of the world and the context we are in to make sense of what is happening. This occurs automatically and unconsciously. This is how the optical illusions above work—they give us key parts of a picture and our brains fill in (or try to fill in) the rest, with very different, sometimes entertaining, and at other times frustrating, results. Further, we know that we can consciously influence what we "see" by what we focus on, but it does not always work very well.

Similar processes happen whenever we learn something in school. We do not come into a situation as a blank slate or as an empty vessel. Rather, we bring all our experiences, ideas, and emotions to whatever situation we are in and we use these, *mostly unconsciously*, to make sense of new information. And, as we described above, the processes of making sense involve comparing new information to our existing understandings of the world around us and then altering the information, our understandings, or both to create a fit. This is why in science education there is a whole subfield on common misunderstandings about the world around us and how to help students overcome them (see, e.g., Chi et al., 2012; Krall, Lott, & Wymer, 2009; LoPresto & Murrell, 2011; Stein, Larrabee, & Barman, 2008).

Take, for example, one of our favorite science misconceptions—what causes the seasons—and how this misconception or *rightly wrong* thinking about astronomy and heat transfer develops in a bright student with a caring, well-meaning teacher. This process is captured in the documentary *Private Universe* (1987).[2] It is one of the most brilliant presentations of how wrong ideas are learned not just despite, but perhaps even because of, the best intentions of the teacher and student. But, unfortunately, the good intentions are also based on *rightly wrong* thinking about how people learn: that the delivery of facts from the teacher to the student will be understood and remembered by the student in the same form as they were transmitted by the teacher. We know, or should know, that this does not happen. When we act as if it does, we build a dumb idea into poor teaching practices, with sadly predictable bad results.

Here is an example of what happens when educators attempt to get *the right answer into the head of a student* using the wrong model of learning about how concepts work in our process of understanding. *Private Universe* (1987) tells the story of how a smart high school student completely mislearns how the Earth's revolution around the Sun is linked to our four seasons despite the fact that the teacher uses a globe to directly tell the whole class how this happens. The more the student was pressed to describe how the seasons happen, the more convoluted her explanation became as she tried to consciously create a pattern that fit all the information she had been presented in class with her strong unconscious prototype about things getting hotter as they get closer to a heat source. By the end of the discussion, the student had created an Earth orbit in the shape of a figure eight, which she knew was wrong, but she could think of nothing better to say. The student's final diagram reminded us of the telephone game—she knew the figure eight orbit was almost comically wrong, but that it was the best answer she had.

We are going to stop here for a moment and dig in a bit deeper. Please answer the question yourself: What causes our seasons? If you said something like, it is hotter in the summer because the Earth is closer to the Sun and colder in the winter because it is farther away, then you are not alone. *Private Universe* (1987) opens its story with graduates of Harvard and MIT—all of whom took multiple science courses in these prestigious universities—saying the exact same thing. And they were wrong. We experience seasons based on the tilt of the Earth on its axis. It is summer in the United States when the Northern Hemisphere is angled toward the Sun and thus it is winter at the same time in the Southern Hemisphere because the Southern Hemisphere is then angled away from the Sun. As a result of this tilt angle, the Northern Hemisphere gets more hours of daylight and the angle of the Sun's rays are more direct, so the Northern Hemisphere absorbs more heat and is warmer—that is how summer happens. At the same time, the Southern Hemisphere receives fewer hours of sunlight and the Sun's rays hit it at a less direct angle, so it does not absorb as much heat from the Sun and is colder—that is what we call winter.

So, why did the smart high school student as well as the Harvard and MIT graduates get this simple idea wrong despite having been told the correct answer in school? Because the way seasons happen is different from the way things get hotter in every other aspect of our lives. The closer something gets to a hot object—whether it is you and a campfire or a spaceship and the Sun—the hotter that something becomes. This understanding is simple and intuitive, because we experience it all the time. We learned it so well that it has become something we just know. It has become our prototype of how things get hot.

At the same time, we do not experience the difference in heat that comes from different angles of a light source as often or as directly as we do with heat and distance. As a result, we have not developed a strong prototype of angle and things becoming hotter, and therefore, we have not learned that concept very well. In the words of cognitive science, we have a very active and dominant prototype in our minds about how heat is related to distance and a very weak prototype, if we have one at all, about the relationship of heat to light angle.

Due to our different levels of experience with these ways that heat is transferred, when we experience a new situation involving heat and being hotter or colder or when we hear about one in science class, our minds activate the stronger prototype of this relationship—the one involving distance—and not the weaker prototype—the one involving light energy and angles. The result is that we often think *rightly wrong* about the seasons and ignore the new evidence that is contrary to our dominant prototype, which are the right answers the teacher told us as students involving heat and light and angles. At best, we may store these new right answers in our brain as a separate idea but not revise our understanding into something more complex and sophisticated that encompasses these new right answers we heard about the world.

There is a very important point here about information and learning: We do not view all information equally. We are predisposed toward information that already agrees with what we currently understand and believe. That is, we tend to be more aware of information around us that matches the way we already see the world. We miss, and sometimes actively reject, information that does not match. Informally, this process is sometimes referred to as the "yellow Jeep effect." Before you become interested in buying a yellow Jeep, you did not really notice all of the yellow Jeeps that passed by you every day. Then, once you buy one, you suddenly begin to see them everywhere. The number of yellow Jeeps in the world did not change dramatically, but your awareness of them did. As mentioned previously, in the language of cognitive science, our tendency to ignore evidence that is contrary to our view of the world is known as the Semmelweis Reflex (Arbesman, 2012). The tendency to see and absorb information that adheres to our current worldview is known as Confirmation Bias (Kahneman, 2011). Both of these automatic, unconscious tendencies can be dealt with by our conscious minds, but it is not easy to do.

It also appears that part of the struggle that the bright high school student and her well-meaning teacher in *Private Universe* were having concerned their misconception that we view all information equally. Or, perhaps even more intriguing, the students believed that they could consciously make themselves value what the teacher said more than what they, the students, unconsciously understood about the world. But we know from cognitive science that the exact opposite is true. The recognition of the Semmelweis Reflex has shown that we are predisposed to unconsciously value what we already understand more than new contradictory information. That's another reason that teachers just delivering correct answers to students will likely do little to further the students' understandings.

And learning is not just about constructing isolated understandings of the world. It also involves developing these understandings and related abilities or skills so that we become good or even expert at doing them.

Learning Skills: Practicing Perfect to Become More Expert

Having discussed how we gain understandings, another aspect of what we expect from education is that our schools develop students who are good—or even expert—at important skills and activities. We are not going to delve deeply here into what should or should not be on this list of important skills and how many of them each student should be good at. But we think it is safe to say that most, if not all, people agree that our schools should prepare students to achieve competence or mastery at some combination of skills that will empower them to be economically successful and good citizens as well as healthy and happy in their lives. This list of desired student outcomes would likely include three skill categories:

Concrete everyday skills such as being able to solve basic math
    problems accurately, write coherent texts for various audiences,
    and read for information and pleasure
Common general skills that are forms or aspects of creativity, such as
    critical problem solving and the ability to collaborate with a team
    in order to accomplish desired tasks
In-depth domain skills needed to be anywhere from good to expert
    in a specific area, such as physics, accounting, sports, teaching,
    music, maintenance, construction, hospitality, or farming, to
    name just a tiny fraction of possibilities, whether for employment,
    enjoyment, or both

So, what do we know about how we learn to be good at something? There are three aspects of being very skilled at doing something on which we will focus here:

1. The feeling of "flow" or "being in the zone" that happens when an expert is doing what they are great at;
2. The types of teaching practices that support improvement to the level of ability where expert flow can and does occur; and
3. The unconscious activity in an expert's brain when this "flow" or "being in the zone" is going on.

First of all, what is this feeling of "flow"? In simple terms, it is the ability to do something well so automatically that, at a minimum, we do not have to stop our activity to consciously figure out how to do parts of it and, at best, allows us to be actively and automatically creative. For example, an expert lawyer would need to know the minute legal details of contract law in the area being negotiated to ensure that the final contract is legally sound.

The lawyer would also need to have the strong negotiation skills necessary to creatively manage two parties (or more) so that they can come to an agreed-upon understanding that works for both sides. In other words, the expert lawyer uses both in-depth knowledge of contract law and strong negotiation skills simultaneously to foresee and resolve problems in the midst of the back-and-forth tense flow of negotiations (Lemov, Woolway, Yezzi, & Heath, 2012).

Here is a common example of this level of expertise: reading. Think about how you read or, more precisely, the fact that you now cannot *not* read. Remember the scrambled and missing word activities from earlier? If you are fluent in English, then as soon as you see them, you just start reading them. You do not have to think about it consciously and, in fact, you are so good at reading that it just happens without any conscious activity on your part.

Of course, you could not always read at this level. Up to some point in early elementary school, you probably could not read at all. Then, you *learned to read*. And, then, at some later point, your emphasis changed and you were able to *read to learn* or to imagine whatever the author was trying to communicate to you. In other words, you became an expert reader. You are now someone who can look at words and do the decoding and make meaning so automatically that your mind is able to spend its energy creating ideas and images that go beyond what the words on the page say explicitly. We can become so expert at reading that sometimes, while we are reading, we can find our minds simultaneously and effortlessly wandering to new, tangential ideas as well.

Learning to drive is similar in many ways to learning to read. Up to some point, usually in our teenage years, we could not drive at all. Then, we took driver's education classes or were mentored by a skilled driver and mechanically, consciously learned to connect what we needed to achieve— say, safely turning left at an intersection—to the various individual physical actions necessary to accomplish that: looking both ways to check for gaps in the traffic, lifting our foot off the brake, putting our foot on the gas, spinning the steering wheel, and so on. Initially, we had to consciously think through these activities, sometimes saying them step-by-step, in order to do it right and make a safe left turn. We practiced these activities in a mixture of classroom simulators, school parking lots, quiet side streets, and eventually busy highways, including the on and off ramps. After much practice— well beyond the time when our driver's education class was finished—we became so skilled at driving that we could do the various discrete skills automatically, creatively anticipating and safely responding to all sorts of new situations, usually to such an extent that we can now carry on conversations while we do it. Some people even like to take a drive to relax or to think.

We become such expert drivers that what was once a chore can become the impetus for creativity.

Sport is another area where athletes, especially the more elite athletes at each level, describe how they learn to become so expert at both the minute details of the activities and the context of the contest that everything "slows" down and they automatically adjust and react in the flow of the game. In other words, athletes can do the two things that we want schools to encourage in our students: do the common activities well and be creative together in the heat of the moment. This fit seems pretty natural in sports, as coaching athletes is a form of teaching.

Putting sports coaching and learning side-by-side, Figure 3.3 paraphrases Brian Kelly, the current football coach at Notre Dame, and William Smiley Howell (among other education and training researchers) describing the four generally accepted knowledge and skill progression levels of someone from novice to expert.

Some scholars on expertise include a fifth level, the level of expert teacher. At the fifth level, one has the *conscious competence of unconscious competence*, which has also been called "enlightened competence," "reflective competence," and "chosen conscious competence" (Lindon, 2013, p. 74). This means that an expert teacher has the ability to consciously develop and communicate specific ways to support and enable their students to efficiently progress through the stages of expertise up to the highest level of unconscious competence.

As educators, we think about our own development in the group of skills we call teaching when we think about this development from the most novice skill level of unconscious incompetence to the most expert level of unconscious competence. When we first started teaching, we spent hours each evening prepping the next day's lessons. We wrote out in great detail each activity we wanted the class to do, what we wanted to accomplish, how long each activity should take, possible problems that might get us off task, the ways to get us back on task, and on and on. We were somewhere at the first two skill levels, probably mostly in the conscious incompetence level: We had a pretty accurate idea of what we needed to do to accomplish the goals we had set for our classes, and it took conscious work to set up everything we needed to do to be successful. Initially, we made lots of mistakes, we were not able to predict all the possible ways that things could go wrong, and not all of our solutions were able to keep or get the class back on track. We continued to work at it and we got better. Our work preparation, application in our classes day after day, and reflection enabled us, as the years went by, to start needing less preparation time to have more successful classes. We moved to conscious competence, then to unconscious competence, and ideally, now, to level 5, the conscious competence of unconscious competence.

Figure 3.3. Levels of Progression from Novice to Expert

	Howell	Kelly
Unconscious Incompetence	This is the stage where you are not even aware that you do not have a particular competence.	You know what that is: You don't know that you don't know what it takes to win. You get that blank stare when you say, "Listen, pay attention to detail. Do this right. Go to class. Be on time."
Conscious Incompetence	This is when you know that you want to learn how to do something but you are incompetent at doing it.	You know what Coach wants from you on a daily basis. You now know what the formula is, but you can't do it yet, because you have so many bad habits. You can't seem to finish the drill. You can't seem to pay attention to detail.
Conscious Competence	This is when you can achieve this particular task but you are very conscious about everything you do.	You now know the message, you are able to do it, but it's really hard. It's hard for you to stay on task. That's where great coaching comes in and keeps you focused, keeps you involved in the process. It's not, "Hey, I want to be a champion." Everybody wants to be a champion. What are you going to do about it? Conscious competence is that area where coaches really need to remind their players every single day what it takes to be a champion.
Unconscious Competence	This is when you finally master it and you do not even think about what you have to do, such as when you have learned to ride a bike very successfully.	That's the habit forming; you know what to do, and you know how to do it every single day. You don't have to be reminded about what it takes to win on a consistent basis because it's been instilled in you. It's been instilled by your family, your parents. It's been instilled in this community. It's been instilled by your coaches. When you want to win the championship, when you want to win them all, you need to get to that level of unconscious competence because then it just happens naturally.

Source: Arnold, 2010; Howell, 1986, pp. 22–23

From the study of experts in many fields, we have learned some fundamental guidelines for how to aid people in progressing in their abilities from the first stage of unconscious incompetence to the fourth stage of unconscious competence and even, for some people, to the fifth stage of "conscious competence of unconscious competence." These include the following:

- Deliberate practice in the individual skills and the learning of the minute facts that make up an activity[3] (Lemov, Woolway, Yezzi, & Heath, 2012);
- Deliberate practice and reflection on the big picture of the activity, such as strategy in sports, negotiations and leadership activities, or the actual processes that scientists and teachers use in solving their work problems[4] (Lemov, Woolway, Yezzi, & Heath, 2012; Nater & Gallimore, 2006; Sullivan, 2011; Turley, 2008); and
- Mentored experience in the complete, actual activity itself. Most activities cannot be taught and learned through explicit instruction out of context. Mastering complex activities requires performing intricate, nuanced skills, accessing sophisticated conceptual knowledge, and the ability to put them all together in real time (Gauvain, 2001; Gawande, 2011; Rogoff, 1990, 1998).

And, for nearly every activity—whether it be speaking, reading, driving, playing an instrument, flying an airplane, running a business, or anything else we expect to do well—the process of development to the level of unconscious competence takes years of good, deliberate practice. Ten thousand hours of successful practice is often presented as the minimum amount of time to achieve unconscious competence at the professional level (see, e.g., Ericsson, Krampe, & Tesch-Romer, 1993; Levitin, 2007). At 4 hours a day, 5 days a week, and 50 weeks a year, that would be 10 years of working at something. This also means that effective practice means practicing success: learning activities where mentors, ideally at level five (conscious competence of unconscious competence), teach the effective ways of doing an activity successfully—in other words, good mentoring of good techniques that is varied and spaced over time (see, e.g., Brown, Roediger, & McDaniel, 2014; Nater & Gallimore, 2006).

Finally, research in psychology and neuroscience show that this type of good, deliberate practice—practice that moves our abilities to the expert level—changes how our brains behave and the process of thinking in our acquired areas of expertise (Bascom, 2012; Haier & Jung, 2008; Sawyer, 2011). Taken together, the brain and psychology research support the following ideas about how expert brains operate differently from novice brains when doing activities in an expert's domain:

- Experts are able to focus better than novices because expert brains appear to inhibit brain processes that are not directly related to the task at hand, thereby limiting to some degree the ability of the experts to change their focus away from the task at hand based on other task-irrelevant stimuli (Haier & Jung, 2008; Milton, Solodkin, Hlustik, & Small, 2007; Sawyer, 2011).
- The activation of certain connections are higher in an expert brain than in a novice brain, but the overall activation level of an expert brain is lower than that of a novice. This appears to mean that practice and improvement in ability is due, in part, to the brain becoming more efficient—rather than harder-working—at processing the information needed to successfully perform the domain activities (Haier & Jung, 2008; Milton, Small, & Solodkin, 2004; Milton, Solodkin, Hlustik, & Small, 2007; Sawyer, 2011).
- There is no unique brain area used only for expert activities. Rather, expertise, like creativity in general, involves different activation levels of brain areas that we also use in everyday, more mundane, activities (Sawyer, 2011).

Only a few of these "expert brain" studies have been conducted so far—though the number is growing—and the findings from these studies must be understood with the idea that the differences in brain activation levels measured were often quite small, often as small as a 5% difference (Sawyer, 2011).

So, what is happening in an expert brain that enables it to process an activity so much more proficiently than a novice? Combining the results of the expert brain studies with studies on the role of prototypes and metaphors in our thinking and learning seems to point to this aspect of high-level understandings as key: As we develop expertise in something, we are able to understand and think about the activity in larger chunks, sometimes referred to as "forward models" (Todorov, 2004) and other times "gestalt" understandings[5] (Lakoff & Johnson, 2003). In an article in *Science News* about the cognitive functioning of elite athletes, Dr. Emanuel Todorov, a neuroscientist at the University of Washington, explains these current understandings as applied to elite, professional athletes:

In the heat of the game, athletes have to process the sensory data they're taking in to automatically deliver the best motor response. To save precious time while performing such calculations, the brain builds a virtual representation of the world so it can predict what might happen next, new research finds. Called "forward models," these mental maps allow athletes to preplan "what they want to accomplish and how they're going to accomplish it," says Emanuel Todorov. . . .

Because they provide reference data, previous experiences are essential for crafting forward models. . . . Forward models aren't set entirely in mental stone, however—a good thing, since rarely are multiple scenarios in sport exactly the same. . . . If [a] forward model didn't make use of current sensory information to adjust predictions built on "priors"—the accumulated knowledge of all the topspin shots he has seen before—[an athlete] wouldn't be able to react on the fly when something unexpected happens. . . .

The brain's predictive machinery is constantly being updated with new sensory information as it executes a motion, a feedback loop that helps the body maintain control over its movement, Todorov says. "Given your goal, given where you currently are, the optimal feedback loop posits the best way to get there," he says.

Todorov and other scientists are finding that athletes' brains calibrate forward models in a manner consistent with Bayesian decision theory, a statistical approach that combines a continual stream of new information with previous beliefs. Because there is a level of uncertainty associated with sensory input, the brain has to decide whether it is going to rely more on the new data (which could be misleading) or on more credible (albeit potentially outdated) priors. Elite athletes, who have acquired more priors through frequent competition and practice and who have less noise in their sensory input and motor output, will have the edge, Todorov suggests. (Bascom, 2012, pp. 26–27)

These examples of the latest brain research show that these models our minds create are essentially gestalt understandings of larger chunks of an activity. They are types of the prototypes and metaphors presented at the beginning of this chapter. These forward or gestalt models enable an expert to understand and think about an activity as larger, cohesive parts—say as a musical phrase rather than individual notes, a chessboard position as a geometric pattern rather than a collection of individual pieces, or a golf swing as one full motion rather individual movements of the arms, hips, and legs. Expert brains are more efficient than novice brains because they can see large chunks of an activity as a single concept (Todorov, 2004). Expert brains do not process a longer list of information faster than a novice brain—in other words, they do not "outwork" a novice brain—but instead, where a novice brain processes a list of steps (a slow, tedious process), an expert brain processes some or all of these steps as one or multiple larger, single concepts (a fast, efficient process). These larger conceptual understandings enable an expert to experience an activity not only more quickly but also at a more in-depth level (Bascom, 2012). In other words, experts have improved the accuracy and depth of their fast-thinking processes.

In sports, athletes talk about the game slowing down when they are able to see larger and larger parts of the field all at once. Chess grand masters describe this ability as seeing the piece positions in geometric patterned blocks. These gestalt understandings—prototypes of the patterns within a block of information—enable experts both to know where to focus their attention within this larger field as well as to focus more deeply into the details of the field, which results in faster decisions, more precise actions, and thus more successful ones.[6]

The fact that our brains shape information into patterned models, including prototypes and metaphors, may be why real-world experience is a key to learning something at an expert level. You cannot become fluent in a foreign language, for example, through classes or computer language programs alone. You need to be immersed in the language at some point to become an expert in it. This may be due to the fact that because our brains process information more efficiently through the use of gestalt models rather than long lists of steps, we need to learn this way as well. Our brains at the unconscious level automatically create these gestalt patterns in order to improve our ability. Too much emphasis on explicit step-by-step instructions or the delivery of lots of *the right answers* can actually hinder our development because it goes against the way our brains operate. In other words, the standard ways of thinking about the learning process that currently dominate our factory model–based educationalese lead to teaching practices that can actually hinder learning!

Finally, we want to make one more important point about learning. We don't learn just what we are taught. We learn everything that we experience. For example, students don't just learn how to divide fractions in math class. They also learn what math and school are supposed to be about and how they as students and people fit in. We automatically and unconsciously create prototypes and metaphors in order to understand these aspects of our world and we attach emotional markers to them in order to prioritize automatically which of the many and sometimes contradictory ones to pay attention to (Damasio, 1999; LeDoux, 1999). Students will walk away from math class, for example, with understandings about how cool or boring math is, about how good at it they are, and how important it is (or isn't) to who they are right now and who they want to be tomorrow. All these understandings are experienced quickly through emotional responses such as "hating" or "loving" math. What we want to highlight is that we learn a whole lot from school and only part of what we learn is the subject matter being taught by the teacher.

In sum, we now know that learning involves the creation of knowledge and skills, often through gestalt models of how the world and our activities in it work, including the specific use of prototypes and metaphors. These models develop into and also from our current state of understandings of the world and our brains develop them automatically, mostly at the unconscious, fast-thinking level. We are never a blank slate. We also know that learning, including practice, changes the structures of our brains in such a way that expert brains operate more efficiently than novice brains by creating accurate models of larger patterns of the world rather than processing more individual steps faster.

Given the research evidence on how we actually learn, we need to move away from the inaccurate CONDUIT and EMPTY VESSEL metaphors and the strict authority-based prototype of the SCHOOL is a FAMILY metaphor and toward more accurate fast-thinking metaphors and prototypes that we can use in the heat of the moment and that will also inform our slow thinking as we decide on and promote evidence-based education reforms. It seems likely that the current educationalese based on these metaphors and the related homogeneous school prototypes have led us to believe in the effectiveness of reforms without any real evidence that they will work, such as the belief that the new Common Core State Standards alone will improve student achievement, and even to believe in them despite strong contrary evidence, such as NAEP test scores, that much, if not all, of the StudentsFirst policy agenda, which includes content-focused alternative certification, vouchers and charters, and larger class sizes, is likely ineffective.

So, where do we go? We contend that we should develop our fast and slow thinking with the LEARNING is GROWTH metaphor and the caring nurturance–based prototype for the SCHOOL is a FAMILY metaphor because they are the closest approximations to how we actually learn and should teach. We describe this thinking and the resulting education model in more detail in Chapter 4.

The GROWTH Metaphors and the Transaction Classroom: More Accurate and Less Prevalent

In this chapter, we describe the LEARNING is GROWTH metaphor for understanding how we learn and should teach (and persuade) and their relationship to the caring nurturance–based prototype for the SCHOOL is a FAMILY metaphor. The GROWTH metaphors more accurately represent how people actually learn than the EMPTY VESSEL and CONDUIT metaphors, though the GROWTH metaphors are still an imperfect approximation.

It is not clear who first began to formally describe and analyze the GROWTH metaphors for learning. We do know, for example, that Herbert Kliebard described the GROWTH metaphors in 1975 in his book chapter, "Metaphorical Roots of Curriculum Design." Over the subsequent decades, researchers, including the authors, have continued to examine the structure, use, and impact of the GROWTH metaphors on how we understand and do learning and teaching (Baptist, 2002; Berendt, 2008; Botha, 2009; Haas, 2007a, 2007b, 2008; May & Short, 2003; Sfard, 2009).

The LEARNING is GROWTH metaphor is composed of two primary metaphors:

- MINDS (or BRAINS) are SOIL.
- IDEAS and UNDERSTANDINGS (and sometimes STUDENTS) are PLANTS.

Like the CONDUIT and EMPTY VESSEL metaphors, we use the GROWTH metaphors in some common types of statements about education. These examples should sound familiar and make sense to you:

"Sean really blossomed in 5th grade."
"I want to plant the idea that she can be a scientist someday."

"Sandra's understanding of math really shot up in high school."
"Ethan has a fertile imagination."
"I enjoyed watching David's growth this year in English."

The logic of the LEARNING is GROWTH metaphor is based on two key ideas. First, people develop or construct their ideas and understandings. People will experience the same words and activities differently and thus will create different understandings. This happens because we construct what we learn from an experience based, in part, on who we are and what we already know and believe.

Second, people need support to help them construct accurate understandings. People need physical and emotional supports—such as food, medical care, safety, and opportunity—so they can do the difficult work of examining what they already know and developing more sophisticated understandings based on the new information and ideas they are experiencing. People also need knowledgeable teachers who can guide their learning with information and activities that will promote the learning process. These teachers help students actively reflect on their current knowledge and wrestle with new knowledge to create more sophisticated understandings.

At a deeper level, we all are shaped by our social contexts and learn through "social modeling." As small children, we observe our adult caregivers in order to learn how to do the most basic things—such as how to hold a spoon or tie our shoes. Social modeling is the process of discovering patterns in the behaviors of others to guide our own actions. It is fundamental to the way every person learns throughout life. And, it supports the use of the GROWTH metaphor by drawing attention to the ecological nature of the learning process. Social environments shape the human minds embedded within them. For example, a child of European descent may observe the use of forks and knives at the dinner table while another child living in China watches all the adults handle chopsticks. Just as a tomato requires certain kinds of soil and climatic conditions to grow and bear delicious fruit, so the logic goes that a person requires certain kinds of social guidance and cultural settings, as well as material supports, to learn the skills that are commonplace in his or her particular society.

The caring nurturance–based prototype of the NATION and SCHOOLS are FAMILIES metaphor is the moral foundation of the LEARNING is GROWTH metaphor of learning and teaching, and this prototype has a different set of foundational understandings from the strict authority-based prototype associated with the CONDUIT and EMPTY VESSEL metaphors. The caring nurturance–based prototype is built on the idea that fundamental truths are not timeless but instead are created through interactions among people and maintained through supportive relationships. The first obligation of the caring nurturance–based family is to provide the supports that people need to develop as individuals and members of a community. Through supportive relational experiences, people will develop an understanding of what it takes to be an interdependent family and will follow communal rules because they work to achieve a shared prosperity. Schools that follow the caring nurturance–based prototype prioritize processes over prescribed content, looking to create experiences where students can live, question, and construct their individual understandings of subject-matter content, including its social implications. Successful students are those who live and learn by a code and process that they can justify as healthy and supportive.

What does the logic of GROWTH metaphors say about teaching and learning? What is a GROWTH model of education that incorporates the caring nurturance–based prototype of the SCHOOL is a FAMILY metaphor and the FREEDOM is SUPPORT metaphor? In sum, it says that teaching and learning are cooperative activities, a transaction between the teacher and the students as well as whatever is being studied. Learning takes place as a student (or anyone) internalizes and reshapes information and experiences into new understandings. Teachers can promote ideas and provide sustenance—resources and learning experiences that promote understanding—but they cannot deliver or force specific understandings. Each student will develop his or her understandings at different rates, times, and in different ways. Although learning cannot be mandated so that all students develop according to the same schedule or through the same process, there are ways that learning can be more effectively invited and enhanced. Thus, as research on student resilience consistently shows, teaching involves nurturing students (Benard, 2004; Truebridge, 2013). Specifically, resilience research shows that for students to be able to do the difficult work of becoming more expert in the subjects they study, they need at least three foundational supports:

1. There must be the expectation that they can achieve at high levels.
2. They must have the material supports necessary to achieve those expectations.
3. They must have meaningful relationships with caring adults to help them develop the emotional and intellectual strength to weather the storms along the way (Benard, 2004; Truebridge, 2013).

This means that a teacher must be able to understand his or her students' needs as individuals and provide a rich, and sometimes individually tailored, environment in which each student can grapple with and eventually internalize a new, more sophisticated understanding of what he or she is studying (Truebridge, 2013). (We will describe some specific examples in Chapter 5.)

Like a plant, a student's understanding will thrive when he or she gets attention tailored to his or her individual needs, as well as strengths and interests.

Understanding teaching and learning with the GROWTH metaphors means that you would assess student learning differently from the standardized tests and repetition of class activities that only make sense when thinking with the CONDUIT and EMPTY VESSEL metaphors. The teacher does not expect what she does or says to be absorbed directly by the students. Rather, like the air, soil, and water that a plant converts into its green structures, students construct and develop their knowledge from the resources and experiences provided to them by the teacher. As a result, student understandings, at least initially, may be different from exactly what the teacher taught (Bachtold, 2013; Brooks & Brooks, 1993). Thus, to ensure that the students are progressing toward the expected accurate and more expert understandings and skills, the teacher and students must continuously assess and communicate about lesson goals and student progress, and regularly adjust the learning activities. Further, it then makes sense to assess learning holistically, using projects and real-life activities and descriptions of progress (intellectual "growth"), as much as possible. These assessments are integrated into each student's learning activities, rather than being done as an external process, by and for others. With the GROWTH metaphors, as opposed to the CONDUIT and EMPTY VESSEL metaphors, the teacher is more likely to be a "guide on the side, rather than a sage on the stage."

Given the interactive and individual nature of learning as understood with the GROWTH metaphors, standardized tests—although useful as part of a repertoire of assessment tools—are not the only or even primary measures of program quality and success. Learning success is measured by satisfaction in one's progress, one's love of learning, and the quality of individual, real-life projects done by the students. In fact, too much emphasis on tests, especially standardized tests, gets in the way of learning—as one anti–standardized test saying goes, measuring corn more often does not make it grow any faster.

Given the emphasis on individual growth and the interaction between a knowledgeable teacher and the student, those who advocate for education with the GROWTH metaphors in mind want more resources put into professional development for educators and for individual student support, including resources to develop more individual education plans for all students as well as more money for school breakfast and lunch programs. These are seen as more important than prepackaged curricula and standardized tests. The caring nurturance–based prototype of the SCHOOL is a FAMILY metaphor and the FREEDOM is SUPPORT metaphor provide the moral and logical foundation for education models based on the GROWTH metaphors: People need safe and supportive schools and communities (U.S. Department of Education, 2014)—from basic food and medical care to computer and lab equipment as well as caring adult role models—to develop to their full potential as both individuals and members of the society, and so we must provide them.[1] This is the right *and* smart thing to do.

What might this type of education support look like? Schools, together with the community at large, should provide some basic supports as public services. Schools, for example, could act as community centers that provide tutoring and library materials, and possibly food and health services. Social and economic programs that ensure the prosperity of all members of the community go hand in hand with education policies. In other words, students need the input of basic resources to survive and thrive.

Thinking with GROWTH metaphors, teachers must be able to facilitate the knowledge construction of their students. This level of skill requires extensive training.[2] To do this, teachers must learn to be experts in their subject matter, learning theory, and pedagogy, because they must develop and manage real, meaningful learning activities that include an emphasis on exploration, open-ended problem solving, and explanation as well as practice in specific skills and techniques. Further, teachers must learn to be flexible and nimble enough in their teaching activities and methods to challenge and support the individual strengths and needs of their students in a group setting. Montessori and Waldorf education, the Citizenship School movement, and performance-based education are examples of programs that emphasize the constructive, GROWTH metaphor understanding of learning and teaching.[3]

There are a number of positive aspects that come from understanding education through the GROWTH metaphors. GROWTH metaphors align well with how people actually learn. These metaphors imply that individuals learn something that is different, though possibly similar, to what a teacher teaches. Further, people are understood as individuals who learn differently because they have unique understandings, both conscious and unconscious, that they bring to each learning activity. As a result, these unique understandings must be elicited and wrestled with by learners if they are to learn what is intended. If this elicitation and wrestling had been done in the *Private Universe* example, then the student would likely not have come away with the misunderstandings about the seasons that she did.

Thinking with GROWTH metaphors, here is a way that a teacher might more effectively teach students about the seasons. The teacher's goal should be to evoke the elicitation and concept wrestling that will be more in line with how people learn and thus be more effective in enabling students to construct accurate understandings than the transmission of right answers by the teacher as understood when thinking with the CONDUIT and EMPTY VESSEL metaphors.

First, the teacher should get students to confront what they already know. This can be done with statements or questions, including ones as simple and direct as, "What causes our seasons to happen?" or "It is autumn right now. Ask questions that you want to know about autumn and the other seasons."

Second, the teacher should create some problems or questions—some cognitive dissonance—that requires the students to compare their understandings with what the teacher knows to be accurate information about the seasons and how they are created. Some of the problems might come from the student questions themselves, with the teacher filling in gaps based on her understanding of the key concepts. For example, the teacher might ask how it can be winter in the Northern Hemisphere and summer in the Southern Hemisphere at the same time or why the days are shorter in winter than in the summer.

Third, the teacher should guide activities that will help students resolve the cognitive dissonance that the questions and problems created. This can be done through various combinations of information-searching activities, including using the Internet, and research activities, such as experiments that mimic or isolate aspects of how our seasons occur. A simple research activity could be to measure the differences in temperature that a single light source will cause to blocks of wood cut at different angles. This activity can be used to demonstrate how the angle at which light hits an object relates to the extent to which it heats it up, part of what occurs as the Earth's angle to the Sun changes through its yearly revolution and the changing seasons.

Finally, during all these activities there is lots of student discussion, guided by the teacher, to enable students to practice and improve their explanations of the various physical phenomena they are examining. Through these regular discussions, students can directly improve their understanding of key concepts and the teacher can monitor their progress. In Chapter 5, we discuss in more detail how an effective math lesson can be built on GROWTH metaphor concepts.

There are, however, limitations to the GROWTH metaphors. Educators who take the individual nature of the GROWTH metaphors too far can become overly focused on "learner-centered" education, where it is presumed that students' curiosity and drive alone will allow them to learn all they need to know. Unfortunately, students cannot know the full extent of what they do not know already or each time they are engaged in *rightly wrong* thinking, and so students need expert mentors to guide them in learning what they need to know and the best ways to learn it accurately. As we demonstrated in the previous chapters, what may seem right to us about how we learn and how the world works is not always so. There are right and wrong answers, and learning takes guided practice and hard work. These ideas can get lost when GROWTH metaphors are taken so far that we suspend all critical judgment and value every individual interpretation as equally valid or by promoting essentialist ideas that individual growth does not mean change, but merely uncovering the person the learner was born to be. The constructive nature of learning and processing information means that we construct ourselves as well.

By this time, we hope that we have made the point that the predominant, almost commonsense way or educationalese in which we understand learning and teaching is based on the inaccurate CONDUIT and EMPTY VESSEL metaphors combined with the strict, authority-based prototype of the SCHOOL is a FAMILY metaphor and the overreliance on the FREEDOM is LACK OF CONSTRAINT metaphor. Further, many of us also can understand learning and teaching through the LEARNING is GROWTH metaphors, the caring nurturance–based prototype, and the FREEDOM is SUPPORT metaphor. But, because these are secondary understandings in our current education discourse, we are often uncomfortable thinking and talking about education this way, even though these metaphors more closely align with how we actually learn. If we are going to improve the U.S. education system, we will need to change how we think and talk about teaching and learning.

Changing how we think and talk about education—incorporating more of the GROWTH metaphors to promote their logic, while eliminating our use of the CONDUIT and EMPTY VESSEL metaphors to limit their logic—will take hard work and practice. In the next chapter, we will apply these metaphors to a number of education issues to explore how we can improve our fast and slow thinking to become more effective at identifying and promoting evidence-based education reforms and thus improve the achievement of our students.

CHAPTER 5

Putting Smarter Fast and Slow Thinking into Practice

Where do we go from here? How do we use what we know about how people learn to enable us to be better at identifying and promoting effective education policies and practices? In other words, how do we enable people to think outside of the models of the current educationalese to envision and understand more effective education reforms?

There appears to be general agreement that 21st-century education should enable students to be successful in college or career choices and to be good citizens (Baldassare, Bonner, Petek, & Shrestha, 2013),[1] which is sometimes described as developing students who are equipped to be productive members of society. We also know from opinion polls (Gallup Poll, 2013) that most of the U.S. public, as well as many educators, politicians, and other education practitioners and policymakers, believe that the current policies and practices will not get us to these results. Education historian Diane Ravitch of New York University sums it up this way in her book *Reign of Error* (2013a):

> We cheat children when we do not give them the chance to learn more than basic skills. We cheat them when we evaluate them by standardized tests. We undervalue them when we turn them into data points.
>
> If we mean to educate them, we must recognize that all children deserve a full liberal education. All children need the chance to develop their individual talents. And all need the opportunity to learn the skills of working and playing and singing with others. Whatever the careers of the twenty-first century may be, they are likely to require creativity, thoughtfulness, and the capacity for social interaction and personal initiative, not simply routine skills. All children need to be prepared as citizens to participate in a democratic society. A democratic society cannot afford to limit the skills and knowledge of a liberal education only to children of privilege and good fortune. (p. 241)

From our work with students and educators, we also believe that most people are comfortable with the CONDUIT and EMPTY VESSEL metaphors and prototypes of homogeneous, strict, authority-based classrooms and so they believe that the resulting transmission style of teaching is the most natural and effective form of teaching (Smagorinsky, Jakubiak, & Moore, 2008). If the dominant prototype for education is that the CONDUIT and EMPTY VESSEL metaphors represent how teaching and learning should be, if it is not working for any given school or student, the fast unconscious response is to assign blame to an ineffective transmission from the teacher or ineffective reception from the student, not the result of misunderstandings of how learning occurs and a faulty way of teaching (Sawyer, 2011).[2] We also believe that the predominant fast thinking about freedom is with the metaphor of a lack of constraint, but most of us are also "slowly" thankful for all the infrastructure that supposedly "restrains" us, while providing supports that enable us to live our lives free of ignorance, danger, and disease, such as public schools, firefighters, police, the Federal Drug Administration, and Medicare (Lakoff, 2007, 2008).

Taking all this together, we see a disconnect between what people want from education and our understanding of how to achieve it. Professor Larry Cuban (2013a, 2013b) of Stanford University describes how preconceptions limit our ability to effectively manage our education problems using the example of age-graded and ungraded schools. To Cuban, the notion of predominant models of age-graded schools as the natural way to organize students, even though age-graded schools do not correspond to the different rates at which each child learns or grows in understanding, stifles effective reform:

> Dominant social beliefs of parents and educators about a "real" school, that is, one where children learn to read in 1st grade, receive report cards, and get promoted have politically narrowed reform options in transforming schools. . . . [To change this dynamic], the age-graded school has to be seen anew as the problem to be solved, not teacher unions, insufficient iPads, or policies that instill fear into teachers or tighten standards-based testing. Ungrading schools create different structures for students to learn at their different paces, reducing dropouts while giving teachers time and flexibility to teach what has to be taught. (2013b, para. 15–16)

The question, then, is how do we align our desires for education with what we know about what is most effective for achieving it?

The key to effective reform is to recognize the limits of our current pedagogical imagination or educationalese because they lead us to focus on the wrong aspects of schooling as the problems and thus the wrong actions for solutions. Unfortunately, these models are not only common and in-accurate, but also powerful. As Yale professor Dan Kahan and his team point out, our preconceived ideas about political issues will trump the facts on policy effectiveness (Kahan, Peters, Dawson, & Slovic, 2013). With all this in mind, it appears that to effectively identify and promote education changes that will result in real improvements in student learning, we will need to explore three coordinated actions.

First, it is important to insist on the relevance of presenting data on what is working in education. Fortunately, there are many committed re-searchers disseminating rigorous research on what is working (and what is not) in education (see, e.g., Berliner, Glass, & Associates, 2014). However, education reform will require more than the delivery of our own facts, our own *right answers* about how the brain works, effective education practices, and evidence that the current system is not working. These are all necessary, but they are not sufficient (Kumashiro, 2008; Philips, 2014).

Second, it is key to actively and explicitly work to understand and ad-dress the relationships between the fast- and slow-thinking models we have about learning and schooling in order to be aware of how to make our facts and our right answers more consciously powerful and persuasive. We must directly call out the models that are wrong and promote the ones that are more accurate. If we do not, then we risk having our comfortable misper-ceptions about learning, teaching, and schooling continue to trump what data and research tell us is effective. But even this is not enough, because discussion is only one part of how we learn.

Third, and perhaps most important, we need to work to implement ef-fective education reforms so that we can directly live them. We need experi-ence with effective education because we are experiential learners.

We want to propose two organizing principles for improving our ability to align our fast- and slow-thinking understandings of learning, teaching, and schools with policies and practices that will be more effective in achiev-ing this learning.

A) The CONDUIT and EMPTY VESSEL metaphors of learning are wrong and misguide educational policies. As a result, education reforms that tweak around the edges of the CONDUIT and EMPTY VESSEL metaphors will not produce real im-provements. The inaccuracy of the CONDUIT and EMPTY VESSEL metaphors means that the many common conceptions of education are inaccurate as well. For example, the prototype of orderly, homogeneous classrooms where the teacher delivers information from the front of the room as the natural and best structure for learning is a dumb idea. As a result, seeking to improve or perfect this type of teaching will not work—another dumb idea. You cannot tweak your way out of an education model that is funda-mentally flawed. You cannot improve and scale up this "sage on the stage" *right answer* delivery model of teaching to enable students to learn in a way where they can apply that knowledge in a new situation. You cannot make *the right answer* delivery into knowledge construction through step-by-step scripted teacher-proof lessons—though people have implemented scripted lessons for years in all sorts of situations (Schoenbach, Greenleaf, & Murphy, 2012; Shanton & Valenzuela, 2005).[3] Likewise, changing the delivery method from teachers to textbooks or videos or the Internet, or through iPads or anything else, also will not work. Technology will not improve student learning if it is only used to make *right answer* delivery more efficient, such as replacing a "pile of textbooks" with an iPad (Bilton, 2010; Cuban, 2003, 2013a).

These ideas will not work because they cannot work. There is no way to mass-produce and deliver learning; that is simply a dumb idea. It is dumb because it is impossible to mass-deliver learning, as we do not learn through *right answer* delivery. We learn through the construction of our experiences into models of the world. Each person must do the work of learning themselves;[4] we can (and must) invite and enable student learning and knowledge development, but we cannot deliver it.

B) The GROWTH metaphor is a good approximation of how people learn. We should use it to guide and check our approaches to improvement. People learn by mentally constructing and reconstructing models of the world (Bachtold, 2013; Brooks & Brooks, 1993; Lakoff, 1987). The learning process is individual, experience-based, automatic, continual, and unconscious, as well as conscious and deliberative. Learning thrives on complexity, dissonance, reflection, interactive explanation, and also practice. We can foster learning, but we cannot deliver or mandate exactly what people learn.[5] We often create models and understandings that are wrong, unexpected, and unknown even to ourselves, and so effective education requires guided individual reflection of our current understanding.

If we start our work in education policy and practice with the concept of learning as individual growth, then we are starting with a more accurate understanding of how people learn. We must explicitly and repeatedly promote individual growth-related concepts of education and even the GROWTH metaphor itself in our work. Further, we must promote the supporting conceptual understandings as well, including new prototypes of what effective learning activities look like—which will probably involve group-work, multiage groupings, open-ended project-based learning, flipped and non-classroom settings, and video simulations, among others (see, e.g., Brame, 2013; Cuban, 2013a, 2013b; Gee, 2007; Stanford Center for Assessment, Learning, and Equity [SCALE], 2013)—and the additional metaphor for FREEDOM as SUPPORT that will enable us to be free from ignorance through education, among other freedoms (Lakoff, 2007).

We must continually remind ourselves that our learning metaphors—including the GROWTH metaphor—are approximations; they are never perfect understandings of the complex and often unconscious learning processes. We can take any metaphor and the resulting education model too far by not venturing outside its internal logic and presumptions to become *rightly wrong*. This is certainly happening now with the CONDUIT and EMPTY VESSEL metaphor misconceptions that support our current focus on transmitting *right answers*. It can also happen with GROWTH metaphor–based education models that do not challenge and guide the learning that students produce. We must, therefore, be conscious and reflective, regularly testing our presumptions and actions against evidence.

To continue pursuing ideas that feel comfortable even though our best evidence contradicts them is madness (to paraphrase Albert Einstein). We use the acronym MAD as a way to remember to test whether an idea or proposed solution that feels right within the internal logic of a model is really a bad idea when compared with the evidence. There are three elements to our MADness test, and we should be skeptical of any idea that has one or more of these characteristics:

- Misunderstands how people actually learn
- Is Applied as a magical silver bullet solution
- Disregards (contrary) evidence (consistently and stubbornly!)

Here's a bit more about what we mean when we say that an idea is dumb because it fails our MADness test.

Misunderstands or mistakes how people actually learn: In this book, we describe how learning involves both fast and slow thinking. When we ignore, for example, how prevalent and important the unconscious mind is in how we think, decide, understand, and learn, then policy and practice ideas that do not take the unconscious into consideration will likely be ineffective at reaching our educational goals.

Applied as magical silver bullet solutions: Another element of a likely ineffective (or already ineffective) policy or practice idea is that because it works in one context, it will work for all people and situations, probably for all time. In other words, the program or policy is sufficient in and of itself for educational success. An additional element of this "magical" characteristic is that it requires "perfect, ideal conditions" in order to be effective. When, unavoidably, the promise of the proposed reform does not work, it is easy to find something or somebody that was less than perfect to blame. This characteristic makes ineffective ideas very resilient and resistant to change.

Disregards (contrary) evidence: Reforms, by their nature, are not fully tested, and we cannot say for certain how effective any policy or practice idea will be in enabling us to reach our educational goals. But there will usually be some evidence (and sometimes a lot of evidence) about an idea. It is important for any idea to address this evidence, especially evidence that contradicts its educational promises. It appears to us that ineffective ideas—or better yet, their proponents—rarely do that. Too often, contrary evidence is just ignored. In this sense, ineffective ideas are often always one-dimensional and simplistic. They transform every educational issue into a "simple problem to be solved," now and forever. A simplistic perspective, however, is not the same as presenting a simple approach. Simple approaches can and often do work, even when we are facing complex challenges. Simplistic approaches, on the other hand, never work because they cannot help but ignore everything that is subtle, complex, nuanced, and difficult in teaching and learning (in other words, almost everything that happens in education).

One way of identifying ineffective or dumb policies and practice ideas is to look for traces of MADness by asking questions and providing straightforward answers.

To connect educational policies and practices with how people actually learn (**M**), rather than how we think they should learn, we could ask:

- How do we understand how people learn?
- Is our understanding of how people learn accurate ("accurate" as described by the best available research)?
- Is our idea for a policy or practice consistent with an accurate understanding of how people actually learn?

To determine whether we are overpromising the impact of any idea by promoting a silver bullet effect (**A**), we could ask:

- What conditions do we need for this idea to be successful?
- Do we need "ideal" conditions, such as perfect students, families, teachers, or society, for our education idea to succeed as promised?
- To what extent will the solution enable us to successfully manage changes in context?

And, to ensure that we are considering the best evidence to enable us to look beyond the internal logic of the education model itself (**D**), we could ask:

- What evidence is available about the likely impact of this idea when put into practice?

- How comprehensive is the evidence for success or failure?
- How does any research or evaluation consider the multiple, simultaneous influences on student learning?

If we cannot answer and defend our answers with links to how a reform builds on how people learn and data that support a likelihood of success, then our policy or practice idea will likely be ineffective and will lead—or, we argue, *has* led—to students who will not be the successful 21st-century individuals we intend. In other words, it is a MAD idea.

Given our tendencies toward MADness—staying within the comfort of the internal logic of any model of education despite, or even because of, evidence that a policy or practice is not working—we strongly urge people to use the MAD framework to guide reform deliberations and the way we promote effective policies and practices.

To emphasize the importance of actively using the MADness framework, we want to revisit the persuasive power of the internal logic of the CONDUIT and EMPTY VESSEL education model. We have described how this model is a misconception of the way people learn, how there is strong evidence that it is not working, and how it still continues to be the predominant way people think about education, including how most people understand the problems and solutions for our education woes. So, we ask again, why does the inaccurate and ineffective *right answer* transmission model of teaching based on the CONDUIT and EMPTY VESSEL metaphors make sense anyway?

There are three reasons we have already presented that relate to the metaphors and our cognitive biases and four others that we have not yet introduced that are very relevant when thinking about educational policymaking. We will summarize the familiar reasons and then present the new ones. First, *right answer* delivery teaching makes sense to us because it is familiar: This is how nearly everyone was taught, so there is an emotional, gut-level response that this is natural and so it must be right, even if it is difficult or ineffectual.

Second, some students will be able to figure out how to succeed in this type of schooling and some will even be able to get some larger meaning— the high-flyer or fast-runner students—despite the lack of learning activities to help them do so. Thinking with the CONDUIT and EMPTY VESSEL metaphors, the logic will be something like this: See; these students can get it, so you can do it, too, since learning really only involves storing the right answers in your head.

Third, and perhaps most subtly powerful, the CONDUIT and EMPTY VESSEL metaphors of learning and the resulting transmission form of teaching is prevalent and comfortable because it feels like it works. We can consciously realize that learning is actively constructed, not delivered to passive absorbers, but because we communicate so quickly and so often in our daily lives, learning still usually feels, at least initially, like it involves information going directly into our brains.

There are four additional reasons that make teaching based on the CONDUIT and EMPTY VESSEL metaphors very appealing to many people, especially those who are in charge of policy decisions in education.

First, in the education model based on the CONDUIT and EMPTY VESSEL metaphors, all learning is measurable, quantifiable, scalable, and can be structured in sequential and predictable ways. For those reasons, it offers the illusion that we are teaching and learning timeless Truths through a meritocratic educational system that is orderly and fair. Success anywhere means that success is possible everywhere with sufficient effort, because, again, learning and teaching involve the simple acts of transmitting and storing the right answers.

Second, the CONDUIT and EMPTY VESSEL metaphors fit well with the strict authority-based prototype of the NATION or SCHOOL as FAMILY to justify the national status quo. The unsuccessful are explained away by their supposed insufficient natural ability and lack of effort. Systemic improvements are premised on increasing motivation through punishment and reward, for students, teachers, and schools, and through ongoing measurement precision to better determine who is or is not meeting learning standards. Further, this model can be affordable. It requires very little investment for the unsuccessful to mandate their improvement, while large investment can go toward established technology and educational testing companies for ever more effective delivery of information and the measurement of success and failure.

A third reason is that the CONDUIT and EMPTY VESSEL metaphors, along with the strict, authority-based prototype, allow participants to extend the results of schooling, good or bad, to justify almost every single pressing social issue. Unemployment, poverty, inequalities, violence, drug abuse, teenage pregnancies, corruption—you name it—we can solve all of them with the transmission of more *the right answers* in school along with the right mix of reward and punishment to ensure that they are learned. In other words, more education is best! This phrase seems to be the favorite slogan of any elected politician and a social aspiration that magically will resolve all our social ills. No need to invest in expanding job opportunities, improving the quality of public infrastructure, or in ways to universalize access to health care or similar programs, when more—ambiguously defined—education will do it. More education is always a silver bullet solution, albeit a vacuous one.

Finally, this CONDUIT and EMPTY VESSEL metaphor and the homogeneous, strict authority prototype–based model of education help us all retain a sense of innocence. They support a belief that our schools are the result of a well-thought-out and rational model developed over centuries of civilization that responds naturally to a world that is a level playing field populated by talented and untalented, motivated and unmotivated students and teachers. Success and failure reflect the merit of the participants and the social obligation is to provide the same minimum support to everyone. In believing this, we create a system that we also believe neutrally allows everyone to rise or sink to his or her natural level. We may not succeed in this system, but we have the comfort of knowing that our success or failure is our own responsibility.

In sum, this CONDUIT and EMPTY VESSEL metaphor and the homogeneous, strict authority prototype–based model of education gives a reasonable sense of order to an utterly disorderly world, generates probable explanations to social situations that offend our sensibilities, and allows us to shift the responsibility of a system riddled with unfairness to the most vulnerable populations. If there is any problem, then the *rightly wrong* thinking of this education model has a readily available answer: Give us more of the same right-answer transmission, testing, and punishment that we already have. What a MAD idea!

It is beyond the scope of this book to offer a complete "how-to" guide of interrelated fast and slow learning, but we believe that working toward a growth-centered model of education needs to pay attention to the following.

Provide individual support. To enable students to learn, we need to provide each one of them with the supports needed to construct knowledge. Freedom, then, is more than just getting out of the way. For example, in Finland, economic inequality is near the lowest in the world, approximately one-third of K–12 students are receiving special education services at any given moment, and over 50% of Finnish students receive special education services at some time during their K–12 career (Sahlberg, 2010, 2012a, 2012c, 2013).

Providing individual support to all learners also means to proactively partner with students' families if we want them to have the knowledge, skills, and resources they need to support their sons and daughters both in and out of school.[6] For example, parents will likely need specific training in how to help students succeed in their learning in school and at home, especially with an increase in the use of flipped classrooms where initial exposure to skills and content may occur for students at home through digital media. For example, how can a parent best monitor their child's learning on these more in-depth flipped classroom homework assignments? How can parents best support their child when they struggle? One approach, Academic Parent Teacher Teams, developed by Dr. Maria Paredes of WestEd, could provide the type and level of support that will enable parents to effectively help their children in school (O'Brien, 2012; U.S. Department of Education, 2013).

Providing individual support will likely lead us to focus on different curricula in addition to different class structures and ways of teaching. Four prime examples of curriculum changes come to mind: bilingual education, arts education, project-based learning, and simulation games, including interactive videogames.

One could support bilingual education merely because of the advantages of being multilingual in our increasingly international and interdependent world. But there are also direct advantages of bilingual education that come purely from a growth mindset. There is very consistent research showing that students who are bilingual score higher on tests of metalinguistic awareness, cognitive flexibility, and executive functioning skills than students who speak only one language (Adescope, Lavin, Thompson, & Ungerleider, 2010; Bialystok et al., 2005; Gold et al., 2013; Hernandez, Costa, Fuentes, Vivas, & Galles, 2010; Krizman, Marian, Shook, Skoe, & Kraus, 2012; Mechelli et al., 2004) and bilingualism may also improve student math and reading test scores (Viorica, Anthony, & Schroeder, 2013). Thus, we can assist student achievement in multiple ways by enabling them to learn a second (or third or fourth) language.

As with bilingual education, research shows that students who are able to take arts classes do better in all academic areas than students who do not take arts classes (Cabanac, Perlovsky, Bonnoit-Cabanac, & Cabanac, 2013; Deasy, 2002; Ruppert, 2006).

Knowledge construction that rises to the gestalt understandings of experts will likely need to include the active, complex, and open-ended problem solving that disciplinary experts do as a central part of their work. Research shows that people thrive on these larger, interdisciplinary problems, so a problem-based curriculum can do wonders for the construction of in-depth conceptual knowledge (Pink, 2011). The SCALE project at Stanford University is one example of resources and research related to how best to implement project-based learning as an integrated form of teaching and assessment.[7]

Finally, one aspect of all of these curricular changes is the use of simulation games to enable authentic problem-solving activities within the constraints of a school day. These simulation activities can include role-plays such as Bafa Bafa,[8] interactive virtual science activities,[9] and even forms of computer games (Gee, 2007).[10] Many of these various simulations can allow students to begin to confront and experience the skills and knowledge they need to be successful in real-world activities in a safe environment and with the opportunity for knowledge construction and skill improvement through repeated practice.

Base school structures on student learning, not vice versa. To support this type of individual, student growth–based learning—in this example, building a series of lessons upon an open-ended project—the structure of the school itself will likely need to change. Larry Cuban's promotion of non-age-graded schools can be part of this change. Another part of this change can be flipped classrooms and digital learning, where videos and other web-based content provide initial exposure to the subject matter outside of school, freeing teachers to challenge and guide students in group problem-solving activities when they are together during class time.[11]

The Lindsay Unified School District in California is currently working to implement this type of learning structure districtwide (Banchero, 2014). Lindsay is building a curriculum, assessment, learning activity, professional development, and integrated technology system designed to promote and enable each student to work at his or her own pace. The system includes interdisciplinary, open-ended projects and collaborative problem-solving activities, plus direct practice in developing specific disciplinary skills and content knowledge. The Lindsay Unified School District calls it their "Performance Based System" because "students work at their performance level and advance through the curriculum when they have demonstrated proficiency of the required knowledge or skills."[12] In essence, the district is working to enable all their schools from kindergarten through grade 12 to become non-age-graded. This is a daunting task, indeed, and one that the Lindsay Unified School District supports with near constant reference to individual student growth and how learning styles and timelines are different for every child.[13] There is, for example, a page on the district website devoted specifically to understanding education through a "growth mindset," with resources for teachers, administrators, and parents.[14]

To enable this individual student growth, schooling will likely no longer look like the predominant prototype of separate classrooms of single teachers standing by the whiteboard in front of a room of 30 or more students who are sitting in rows of individual seats doing more or less the same thing. Instead, there will be multiple activities occurring simultaneously that involve various levels of student choice, alternative learning spaces, collaborative work, and technology.

Require and provide in-depth, extensive, experiential teacher training. For teachers to effectively enable individual student learning growth when they are responsible for a group or groups of students within a mass education system and through multiple learning modalities, they must be experts in their disciplines, in learning, and in pedagogy. As we described in the previous chapter, great teachers are level 5 experts, the highest level of expertise there is, who work in a profession that David Berliner (2002a) describes as being harder than that of a rocket scientist.[15] They must be able to use the group setting to their advantage, while also minimizing its limitations. Take, as one example, the teaching of writing and the use of individual teacher conferences and also peer-to-peer reviews and editing. This fits well with our knowledge that students learn best when they grapple with complex literacy activities that involve both multiple opportunities to give and receive feedback and to make revisions. This type of learning structure, however, will not work if you simply add them to a classroom with teachers and students who are accustomed to a teacher being the sage at the front of the classroom and students who sit in rows and do their own work. Rather, the entire class structure will need to change and the teacher and students will need to learn how to function successfully in that type of environment.

Teachers will need to learn how to implement this type of writing classroom. How can one enable teachers, who as students themselves most likely experienced years of schooling where teachers transmitted lots of right answers to the class as a whole, to lead a growth-based classroom that emphasizes open-ended problem solving and explanation? A very effective way is to have teachers experience this type of learning themselves, because, really, that is how we change—by experiencing something new that is successful in all its complexity.

One example of this approach comes from the WRITE Institute, a program that is part of the San Diego County Office of Education.[16] The WRITE Institute staff's aim is to improve student writing by improving teachers' abilities to teach writing through a writer's workshop–type approach. The WRITE Institute works to develop effective writing teachers by developing strong "teachers-as-writers" and teachers as analyzers of student progress. In other words, the WRITE Institute develops teachers' abilities to "teach" writing by enabling the teachers to do and understand what they are asking their students to do in a writer's workshop type of learning structure: to write well and analyze writing well. WRITE Institute curriculum and classroom activities are directly linked to professional development through two foundational activities: teacher modeled writing and group analyses of student writing. Teacher modeled writing entails teachers regularly doing their own personal writing and also doing many of the writing activities that their students do in order to improve their own writing skills and to viscerally understand what writing entails and the experience that their students are going through. Central to this linked professional development and teaching approach is having the teacher model or demonstrate the writing process for the class. The teacher will literally write in front of the class, starting from scratch. This active modeling enables the students to experience more directly the process of how a more experienced and skilled writer actually writes, including mistakes and corrections, in real time.

In addition, groups of teachers regularly meet to assess and discuss student work on common writing assignments, guided by the WRITE Institute staff. This work enables teachers to probe the complexities of what makes good writing, mine the clues that student miscues tell about their current level of skill and understanding,[17] and share effective response activities that have worked in other contexts and how they might be implemented in their own. These teacher critiques of student writing are similar to, though more sophisticated than, the peer-to-peer feedback and editing that the students do in the classroom. The WRITE Institute approach and other similar program approaches are based on how students and teachers learn, and there is evidence that this type of professional development improves teachers' ability to implement these effective practices. There is also evidence that student writing ability improves (see, e.g., Schoenbach, Greenleaf, & Murphy, 2012; Walqui & van Lier, 2010).

Teachers who can optimize student learning in a mass-education system that is growth-centered must be true level 5 teaching experts. And, like experts in any endeavor, expert teachers are made, not born. To become an expert, a teacher will need extensive, high-quality training, years practicing their craft, ongoing coaching from current experts, and the resources to do their job well (Mehta, 2013). As we discussed in the Introduction, the National Board Certification[18] process is a strong attempt both to help develop teachers to the expert level and to recognize that level of expertise that is based in consistent research on its effectiveness in improving student achievement (see, e.g., National Research Council, 2008; Vandervoort, Amrein-Beardsley, & Berliner, 2004).[19] Further, we contend, that National Board Certification success is due in large part to its teacher development process for helping good teachers become expert ones. First, this occurs through the certification process itself, which requires teachers to provide evidence of high-quality teaching along with their reflective analyses as to what made their teaching effective. National Board Certification is an advanced teaching credential. As part of this process, teachers must analyze their teaching context and students' needs, submit videos of their teaching, and provide student work samples that demonstrate growth and achievement. As we described in the Introduction, the reflective analyses that they submit must demonstrate four areas of expertise: a strong command of content; the ability to design appropriate learning experiences that advance student learning; the use of assessments to inform instructional decisionmaking; and the ability to develop and utilize partnerships with colleagues, parents, and the community (National Board for Professional Teaching Standards, 2013a).

Second, the National Board encourages teachers to work collaboratively and to seek out mentoring from teachers who are National Board

Certified. The National Board website provides links for finding local NCBT Networks and other teacher support resources.[20] Given the rigor and growth-based process of National Board Certification, it is not surprising to us that studies have consistently shown that the students of National Board Certified teachers outperform the students of non-NBCTs. Unfortunately, National Board Certification does not appear to fit with the current educationalese that deemphasizes teacher development through rigorous certification training in favor of quick alternative teacher entry programs and only about 100,000 of the current 3 million teachers are National Board certified (National Board, 2013b).

It should, we believe, seem fairly obvious that teacher training programs that attempt to shortcut the expert developmental process by focusing on one or two, but not all three of the teacher skill areas, or by training teachers in a matter of months, rather than years, are unlikely to produce expert teachers. Unfortunately, it often is not obvious. Take, for example, the short-term alternative certification and teacher training program Teach for America (TFA). TFA is a program that seeks to improve student performance by placing recent college graduates in various disciplines for 2 years as K–12 teachers in schools with lots of low-performing students. These recent college graduates were successful students, often in prestigious universities, and TFA gives them about 2 months of training in how students learn and pedagogy before placing them into classrooms, nearly all of which are filled with poor students who have struggled to do well in school.[21]

The theory of TFA is that these successful, content-knowledgeable and high-energy students will be able to step in and improve their students' achievement and simultaneously drive systemic change by their example during their 2-year teaching assignments. For nearly 24 years, TFA has worked to make this happen (Teach for America, 2014). Rigorous, peer-reviewed studies of TFA teachers, however, have shown that they could not do it (Heilig & Jez, 2010, 2014). The students of uncertified TFA teachers generally scored lower than those of certified teachers with similar years of experience who took years of teacher preparation courses (see, e.g., Darling-Hammond, Holtzman, Gatlin, & Heilig, 2005; Heilig & Jez, 2010, 2014).[22] TFA teachers did show greater impacts on student achievement in mathematics once they obtained additional training and certification, usually in their second year of teaching and beyond, but rarely in reading (Heilig & Jez, 2010, 2014). However, TFA turnover is very high—higher than the rate for teachers from teacher preparation programs: Fifty percent of TFA teachers leave during or at the end of their 2-year assignment and a total of 80% leave by the end of 3 years of teaching (Heilig & Jez, 2010). This high turnover rate makes it difficult for schools to build the staff continuity necessary to develop expertise across their faculty.[23] In the executive summary to their 2014 report, Heilig and Jez summarize the findings from peer-reviewed studies on TFA impacts:

> despite hundreds of millions of dollars in funding and extensive lobbying by supporters and prominent alumni, TFA appears to offer few if any benefits for improving teacher quality in hard-to-staff schools. (p. ii)

Taking all the studies, both peer-reviewed and non–peer-reviewed, and viewing them in a light most favorable toward TFA, it appears that after nearly 24 years of effort, students of TFA teachers at times do a bit better than some comparison groups and at times a bit worse, depending on the comparison group, subject matter, and grade level examined. And there does not appear to be any evidence that TFA teachers are causing any systemic improvements to happen in the schools, districts, or states in which they work.

Though we are not aware of studies reporting on direct comparisons between TFA and National Board certified teachers, there is ample evidence that the students of National Board certified teachers score significantly better than those taught by teachers from other preparation models, including alternative certification (Darling-Hammond, 2006; Darling-Hammond, Holtzman, Gatlin, & Heilig, 2005; Darling-Hammond & Sykes, 2003). Despite the research reports indicating its pedagogical weakness (Heilig & Jez, 2010, 2014), TFA continues to receive tens of millions of dollars in support to expand its problematic program, while the National Board struggles to expand its successful one.[24] How could that be? There are many possible explanations, ranging from ideological preferences to genuine desires to improve education, but we also contend that misconceptions linked to the current educationalese factory model play key roles in trumping the research evidence. The content focus of a short-term alternative certification program such as TFA appears to be based on the common CONDUIT and EMPTY VESSEL–based misconception that understanding can be produced in students by transmitting lots of *the right answers* to them. Thus, this logic would say, successful students in a particular content area from a prestigious university would be strong teachers. Further, because learning is framed as students piling up *the right answers* delivered by their teacher, then a good teacher alone will be sufficient to significantly increase students' academic achievement—not just compared with similar students, but also compared with students who have greater resources. And, if the CONDUIT and EMPTY VESSEL metaphors provide an alternative framing for TFA's lack of success, then the blame can go to the students and their families, whom are supposedly just not trying hard enough to succeed.[25]

Great teachers, even those with National Board certification, are necessary but not sufficient for high student achievement. Students also need lots of support to do the hard work of learning. Thus, education reforms that focus only on teachers and schools, such as TFA or new standards and standardized tests, but not the social and economic conditions of students' lives will not work. There is a great deal of research[26] that consistently highlights two contradictory facts about the United States: (1) Family wealth and parent educational level directly impact student academic achievement and (2) the United States does a terrible job of providing the education, economic, and social resources that children and their families need for children to learn to a high level. This contradiction between research evidence and U.S. social policy is often disregarded through the use of the metaphor of FREEDOM as LACK OF CONSTRAINT, built on the further metaphors that our society is a "level playing field" and thus only effort, not family resources, explain and enable success (Shenker-Osorio, 2012). It is the inaccuracy of these two metaphors that makes it so important to reframe the education policy discussion with the GROWTH and FREEDOM as SUPPORT metaphors.

Freedom, when understood only as the absence of constraints, provides indirect support for the misunderstanding that we live in a world where expertise is inherent and found in exceptional individuals or that, at most, simply requires hard work on a level playing field. This is clearly incorrect, but it is a common misconception that is repeatedly broadcast and instilled as a fundamental element of the mythology of the American character. It demonstrates one of the key strengths of the GROWTH metaphor as a guide for reforming actions in education: The GROWTH metaphor keeps us focused on the accurate understanding that freedom also requires the individual resources needed to keep us out of the clutches of harm and ignorance, which will enable us to succeed through hard work. George Lakoff and Glenn Smith (2012) put it well when they state:

> The Public provides freedom. . . . Individualism begins after the roads are built, after individualists have had an education, after medical research has cured their diseases. . . . (para. 3, 30)

The GROWTH metaphor is a good point of departure to promote more effective education reforms: language, experience, thought, and learning are inseparable. We cannot deliver *right answer* reforms, just as we cannot deliver *right answer* knowledge to students. Nor can we expect that politicians, educators, parents, and students will experience an education reform the way we intend. We must advocate the right "thinking points," to quote George Lakoff again, which include both the right ideas and the right language, and implement effective policies and practices so that people can learn through experience as well (2006b). One may slightly lead the other, but both must be understood and implemented as two sides of the same reform coin. This is especially difficult because the CONDUIT and EMPTY VESSEL metaphors, as well as their related prototypes of homogeneous, strict, authority-based classrooms are so predominant in our thinking and culture. And, because reforms take time—there is almost always chaos and ineffectiveness when it comes to a new implementation (Fullan, 2001)— reform implementation must be supported by the right thinking until the experience can actually sustain the thinking.

Fast and slow avoidance of MADness. If we were magicians, we could re-create our prototypes and metaphors of the ideal and natural setting for learning so that our educationalese better aligns with how learning does oc-cur and teaching should occur. But we are not magicians. Instead, the emer-gence of new metaphors and prototypes will need to be actively developed through an experiential, embodied learning process that will be, at times, messy, confusing, disjointed, social, and recursive. It will also need to be focused, reflective, guided, individual, and repetitive. Classroom practices will need to include *both* individual, nonclassroom practice of discrete skills *and* teacher-led, group activities, not either/or. Successful learning activities will follow guidelines that teachers adapt for their students in their own context, not silver bullets rigidly imposed because they work in some way somewhere else. To accomplish these goals of identifying and promoting effective reforms, we will need to align accurate fast and slow thinking, continually using rigorous and multiple types of evidence to as-sess the success of any implementation. We believe the MAD guidelines can support this process.

The use of the MAD guidelines brings us back to three policies that we have addressed to various degrees in the book: (1) the Common Core State Standards (CCSS), (2) the use of student test scores in teacher evaluations (Value-Added Models, VAMs), and (3) charter schools. What evidence sup-ports their likelihood of increasing high student achievement, such as being college and career ready and engaged citizens by high school graduation? And, if these policies are implemented—which all three have been, at differ-ent levels—how can the GROWTH metaphors and related prototypes enable us to make them as successful as possible (presuming, for the moment, that they *can* be made more successful)?

First, we recognize that in order to convince the public and gather the level of political support necessary, educational policies are often presented as *the* solution to particular problems. But even recognizing that there was a bit of exaggeration in the promotion of policies such as CCSS, VAMs, or charter schools, it is time to accept that there is little evidence that they will enable the high levels of student achievement that we desire.[27] Using our guidelines, if these programs are framing learning using the EMPTY VESSEL and CONDUIT metaphors, and are being presented as THE SOLUTION while ignoring contrary evidence, they will just reinforce educationalese and educational MADness.

Second, what can be done? Can these policies be salvaged by adding aspects of other policies and practices that enable the natural process of fast and slow student (and even teacher) knowledge construction? Can we take the limitations of these Common Core State Standards (or any new standards) and develop them into opportunities for better teaching and learning (Hakuta, Santos, & Fang, 2013)? Can we do the same for charter schools and VAMs for teacher evaluations?

Perhaps. One possibility is to leverage these policies to support other policies and practices that already meet the MAD criteria, such as the examples we described above. For example, the Lindsay Unified School District could use the emphasis on student explanation in the CCSS to support the student knowledge construction they are seeking in the balanced use of interdisciplinary, open-ended projects and collaborative problem-solving activities with direct practice in developing specific disciplinary skills and content knowledge in the performance-based system. Or, the WRITE Institute could use the emphasis on literacy across the content areas to motivate secondary teachers to do the hard, but effective, professional development work of learning to be better writers as a means to develop their literacy teaching skills, especially for English language learners at the high school level. Similar approaches can be done for charter schools. For example, educators grounded in the sound GROWTH metaphor–based models of education could use the relative freedom of a charter school to implement more supportive school structures, such as a nongraded or cluster-graded system. We are more skeptical about the usefulness of VAMs, but we believe even they could promote teacher development if they were based on a variety of evidence, deemphasized student test scores, and were used in a formative rather than a summative manner. We would not have made new standards, charter schools, or VAMs based on student test scores the centerpiece of any reform effort, because neither the evidence nor the latest research on how people learn makes them likely to improve student achievement. Our reading is that some good may still be gained from rearticulating them to support GROWTH-based models with existing evidence of effectiveness. In other words, no matter how well devised the policy is or how strong the political support for the initiative, if the educational reform is framed with the metaphors of CONDUIT for learning, FREEDOM as LACK OF CONSTRAINT, and homogenous families as the best setting, the end result will be more of the same: educationalese and MADness.

CHAPTER 6

Conclusion

Photograph by Eli Baden-Lasar

We are the students of today
attending the schools of yesterday
being taught by the teachers of the past
with methods from the Middle Ages
to solve the problems of the future![1]

We present this saying, along with a photograph of some of today's students.[2] The saying's lament is apt: We teach today as if nothing has changed in the past century—not our students, not our society, and not our understanding of the human mind and learning. And then, we blame everything and everyone except the outdated policies and practices when they do not result in students who are economically successful, good citizens, healthy, and happy. How MAD is that?

Can't we do better? We certainly think so.

In this book, we have been making the case for improving education policy and practice by applying what we now know about how we learn and think in these ways:

1. Continually paying attention to the unconscious fast thinking dimensions of learning and teaching in promoting effective policies and practices;
2. Actively abandoning the CONDUIT and EMPTY VESSEL metaphors for learning and promoting the GROWTH metaphors instead; and
3. Managing our tendencies toward the MADness of *rightly wrong* thinking that derives from presuming that the comfortable internal logic of a fast-thinking education model means that it is also an

accurate one, whether that model is built on the CONDUIT and EMPTY VESSEL metaphors or any other.

In sum, we are proposing an added level of analysis and a way of examining education policies and practices to better understand the nagging question that gave origin to this book:

> Why do we continue to promote ineffective ideas about education despite strong evidence that what we are doing to kids, especially in contexts of high poverty, won't help them learn and, at times, may be harming them?

Very likely, most of us will automatically answer this nagging question using some combination of the following:

1. Most people are ignorant or misinformed about how to teach kids.
2. A lot of people are cheap, selfish, mean, or stubborn and don't care about other people's children.
3. In general, schooling is such a complicated and emotionally charged area that people are either confused or irrational about educational issues.

The beauty of these three answers is that they are easy, fast, and, in many cases, accurate responses. We all know a relative, friend, or colleague who is ignorant, selfish, or confused about what really matters about education. However, our understanding of how people think and learn makes it important to consider a fourth response that we introduced at the beginning of the book. When thinking about education and schooling, most people are:

4. *Rightly wrong* because most of us are unconsciously using CONDUIT and EMPTY VESSEL–based models in our fast and even slow thinking about learning, teaching, and schooling.

Moreover, until we abandon the CONDUIT and EMPTY VESSEL–based model, we will most likely continue to repeat ineffective educational ideas. It is the gut-level comfort that results from this *rightly wrong* thinking that enables us to be confident in our educational MADness. We move forward again with ineffective ideas, feeling that we are right for the wrong reasons, and with a wonderful feeling of certainty.

Our claim is not nearly as radical as it may appear at first glance. It is not hard to find historical examples in which the dominant perspectives about very important social issues—from attitudes about gender to the acceptance of slavery—were incorrect and changed dramatically only after being consistently contested. The opposite possibility is also important to consider: Some people maintain their beliefs even when there is nearly universal consensus against their perspectives. What we want to distinguish is that when the best empirical and research evidence points in a certain direction—such as our heliocentric solar system, the relationship between human actions and climate change, the link between smoking and cancer, and the constructive dimensions of learning—people who stubbornly resist the consideration of other alternatives go beyond being *rightly wrong*. In many such cases, people who act in this way are engaging in ideologically motivated and dangerous actions, something that we call being *actively wrong*. As Michel de Montaigne said, there is no superior proof of human stupidity than a stubborn and ardent clinging to one's opinion.

Bringing Montaigne to our discussion is not a casual addition, but instead a recognition of how indebted we are to the thinkers of the Enlightenment and how we want to go beyond some of their perspectives (Lakoff, 2008). The ideas we are presenting propose a rationality that extends the legacy of the ideals of the Enlightenment by incorporating our brains' automatic, unconscious, fast-thinking pattern-making of our lived experiences for figuring out how things work, as much if not more than our current focus on conscious, slow-thinking deliberation on facts and right answers. This is why we emphasize the powerful, prevalent, and generally inaccurate fast-thinking influence of the CONDUIT and EMPTY VESSEL–based model of education and the need to promote the less prevalent but more accurate GROWTH-based model. We are using these models in our fast thinking and they guide our actions and slow-thinking conclusions, though often we are not consciously aware of their influence. We are rational, though in a different way from what most of us imagine.

Going forward, we want to address some of the many questions concerning how to put alternative learning and GROWTH-oriented ideas into practice. In promoting or resisting a particular education reform, most of us will try to determine a winner and loser of the debate, because we are all constantly searching for the right answer to any important issue in life. Ideally, we all would love to have societies based on enlightened and reasonable systems that can always reach consensus based on high-quality data, reasoned justifications that are summarized in pithy statements that will objectively demonstrate that one side is wrong and another is right, followed by an agreed-upon solution. In other words, despite our best slow-thinking resolutions to act according to GROWTH models of learning construction, we still get ourselves caught up in a familiar *right answer* problem-solving mood because the CONDUIT and EMPTY VESSEL–based models of learning and persuasion are the way nearly everyone was taught and the way most of us, at least at the fast-thinking level, discuss, debate, and attempt to persuade.

At the level of persuasion, those who attempt to promote GROWTH model–based education reforms through *right answer* debates can act in a *rightly wrong* manner. Our attempts to persuade by relying primarily on right answers means that our process of persuasion is itself framed within the parameters of the CONDUIT and EMPTY VESSEL metaphors. That is, if we can present a fact that is persuasive to us, then it must, on its face, be persuasive to you. Although we know this is not accurate and even though this is rather apparent when thinking with the GROWTH metaphor for learning, it is also futile and temporary within the parameters of the CONDUIT and EMPTY VESSEL metaphors. To "win" within CONDUIT and EMPTY VESSEL–based thinking, our supporting examples are objective evidence and should have the same persuasive impact on you. However, that thinking soon repeats, and both sides counter-argue back and forth with something like this: We know some students and teachers who, in spite of your argument, have learned and prospered by following my recommendations, and thus, my argument must be right, and yours must be wrong. We know, of course, that these types of arguments rarely, if ever persuade, because, to adapt a common saying, the plural of anecdote is not data, and no matter how compelling I feel my anecdotes are, they are not necessarily compelling data for you.

Clearly, we have a very skeptical perspective about the improvements or lessons to be learned from this type of debate. Are we destined to be moving constantly from disappointment to disappointment when discussing education? We don't think so! We see educators and education advocates attempting to include aspects of a GROWTH-based education model in their thinking and arguments as a positive sign. Our critique of imperfect attempts is to demonstrate what we see as an all-too-common, related shortcoming in the thinking and persuasion of many well-intentioned people who are trying to promote effective change: (1) We can simultaneously think with both the GROWTH metaphor and the CONDUIT and EMPTY VESSEL metaphors, but the CONDUIT and EMPTY VESSEL metaphors often dominate when it really matters, such as when we must think on our feet when attempting to persuade in what is or has become a heated debate; and (2) this is more likely to occur when our GROWTH metaphor understanding is underdeveloped and thus withers when confronted with CONDUIT and EMPTY VESSEL–based counter-arguments.

But let us also be clear: Our current educationalese based on the inaccurate CONDUIT and EMPTY VESSEL models is deep and consistent in our societal discourse and thinking, and the resulting policies and practices that result and are promoted as silver bullets are not just ineffective, but harmful. As we have described throughout this book, the evidence is consistently against the CONDUIT and EMPTY VESSEL–based agendas such as those advocated by Michelle Rhee's StudentsFirst organization (see, e.g., Berliner, Glass, & Associates, 2014; Darling-Hammond, 2010; Ravitch, 2011, 2013a; Sahlberg, 2012a, 2013).[3] And so we must improve our ability to advocate for effective reform ideas in the face of the MADness of *rightly wrong*, and possibly *actively wrong*, ideas.

We resist doubting the intentions of Michelle Rhee and her StudentsFirst organization, though some disagree (Berliner, Glass, & Associates, 2014; Ravitch, 2013a). We also resist doubting the intentions of the possibly millions of people who identify with the StudentsFirst policy agenda. We can give Rhee the benefit of the doubt and believe she wants to contribute to solving the great challenges of education, while we also criticize her ideas as MAD. In other words, we can, and we contend that we should, start with the belief that we disagree with Rhee because she is *rightly wrong,* but we should also consider the possibility that she is *actively wrong*. We must not overlook ignorance, confusion, and the relevance of ideological preferences and power politics, but first and foremost we make efforts to anchor education discussions and actions on accurate understandings of learning. Otherwise, debates about educational issues will continue to be reduced to futile calls for improving our tolerance for the alternative point of view, but evidence will be ignored or even disregarded.

So, what would sensible teaching intended to foster learning, and not mere compliance, look like? What kinds of teaching would likely be effective based on our most current understanding of how we learn, research and data on the effective implementation of these practices, and sensitivity to the diversity and differences across communities, families, schools, classrooms, and students?

As we mentioned in Chapter 5, our guiding principle is to avoid MADness in education, and a logical conclusion of this principle is to frame our suggestions with caution, insisting that we don't believe in silver bullets, but in strong reasoned warrants[4] based on what we consider to be the best available research evidence. In short, we want to stress a set of complementary notions to stop MADness, and in so doing, avoid ineffective ideas about teaching in order to maximize learning.

School reform proposals that ignore poverty and other social inequalities misunderstand the way people learn. Academic achievement has always been linked to access to both school quality and to levels of social, economic, gender, racial, and ethnic equality. It is a CONDUIT and EMPTY VESSEL fallacy that great teaching can, by itself, solve all academic achievement problems and free the millions living in poverty from its grip through a redemptive educational system (Fischman & Diaz, 2013). The freedom to do the hard individual work of high, even expert, levels of learning requires consistent support. If we do not pay simultaneous attention to social and educational inequalities, we will not be able to adequately address the social and educational needs of 21st-century societies. Simply put, learning is knowledge construction, not storage, and so learning takes both individual effort and community-provided resources.

School reform proposals cannot ignore the fact that teaching and learning are fundamentally social activities performed by individuals who are members of communities. Effective teaching that fosters learning cannot ignore individual membership nor presuppose that *all* members of a community will behave in similar and predictable ways. Our society is diverse, and our classrooms should be, too. Diversity is a source of insight and innovation that enables us to live well in our world. We need to move beyond our prototype of familiarity and sameness of classrooms—from people looking the same to students doing the same thing all in a row. Individual knowledge construction of more sophisticated understandings thrives on complexity and the reflective resolution of cognitive dissonance that is inherent in dealing with difference (Fischman & Haas, 2012). Difference should be fostered, not feared.

School reform proposals need to consider the fast- and slow-thinking dimensions of teaching and learning. We all bring some initial, fast-thinking understandings to a new topic, and our fast-thinking understanding should not be ignored. Effective teaching requires that teachers plan to spend time learning what students know at the start and to help students recognize what they already know at the fast-thinking level. This runs contrary to the common practice of the CONDUIT and EMPTY VESSEL–based model, which presumes that everyone starts with the same prior knowledge, or lack of it, as well as a conscious awareness of that knowledge. When students are confronted with problems that recognize their existing fast-thinking understandings, learning is facilitated because teachers can recognize problems and target more specific challenges while validating students' starting points. These teaching concepts are fundamental to the GROWTH-based model, but are contrary to the CONDUIT and EMPTY VESSEL–based model that leaves current or prior knowledge undiscovered and unaddressed and, at worst, treats such knowledge as "ignorant."

The need to explicitly elicit and address current fast-thinking knowledge and understandings on any education issue is equally true of persuasion and advocacy. These two activities must be recognized as forms of teaching and learning with the same need for the facilitated surfacing of current understandings. Being *rightly wrong* is common and must be addressed to aid effective education reforms.

Maximizing learning demands that students practice all aspects of expertise in any given discipline. Students must learn how to solve specific, discrete problems and also practice problem solving itself, including creativity, explanation, and teamwork. In the CONDUIT and EMPTY VESSEL classroom, nearly all learning ends at the attainment of the prespecified *right answer*. More sophisticated skills are left for the future—once the basic right answers are learned—which usually never comes and is contrary—again—to the way people actually learn. Similarly, education reform advocates must work on all aspects of persuasion, including improving their knowledge of their own unconscious fast-thinking understandings, as well as those of people who disagree, and must learn how to bridge that gap. The MADness framework can aid both of these processes.

Motivation to be creative and to reach high levels of achievement is primarily internal (Pink, 2011). Motivation starts with the joy of problem solving and the positive emotional experience of success. Problems are motivating and enable learning when students are given the resources—from the teacher and school and also from society and their families—to meet the challenge of solving them. There is much less need for the less effective and often detrimental common punishment and reward consequences of the CONDUIT and EMPTY VESSEL classrooms. An internal motivation perspective requires an expanded understanding of freedom to include the need for the resources and support that will enable people to do the hard work of learning. Higher standards without the means to achieve them are counterproductive at best and can be crippling to motivation at worst.

Additional resources for education must be appropriately targeted. More schooling and more resources used in the same CONDUIT and EMPTY VESSEL–based education and schooling models will not make learning better.[5] Schools are complex systems that attend to many goals and perform many functions, but we need to make clear that in the 21st-century, "learning" should be the priority and all other functions need to contribute to it. Focusing on the main goal of maximizing learning must include accurate facts about what is really happening. But that is not sufficient, either. Human beings are dual rationalists—we make sense of the world in an ongoing constructive process that involves both continual fast-thinking reactions and the interruptions of our fast-thinking reactions with slow, conscious thought. Effective teaching and effectively promoting fact- and research-based education policies and practices require absolutely that we understand and interact with our fast-thinking models of education—including their fundamental elements of metaphors and prototypes—that we initially express as gut feelings and that may or may not equate with the evidence (Fischman & Haas, 2012; Haas & Fischman, 2010). When our fast-thinking gestalt models align with the evidence and thus inform and align with our slow thinking, we can develop into experts; when they do not, we too often accept the comfort of emotional certainty, to the detriment of effectiveness. We must avoid this tendency to accept comfort as truth.

In the spirit of moving beyond the comfortable, we call on education advocates working to put GROWTH-based reforms into action to get their own houses in order. We want to go beyond easy labeling and hopeful appeals to be tolerant with the good sense of opposing arguments in education debates. We believe that the evidence is clear and consistent: There are better pedagogical options than the CONDUIT and EMPTY VESSEL–based education system. To develop these better options, a first step for those who advocate for more accurate GROWTH-based education models is to be able to articulate well the foundations of human learning that will drive the structure, activities, and content of this more effective education system. We can neither inadvertently reinforce predominant but inaccurate versions of key contested concepts, such as learning and freedom, nor can we fumble our discussion points once we have set the debate.

Unfortunately, many of the current debates are among different *rightly wrong* positions that have the appearance of diverse educational perspectives, but their differences are more ideological than pedagogical. Debates about schooling among people using different forms of *rightly wrong* arguments organized by the CONDUIT and EMPTY VESSEL metaphors for learning and the homogeneous, strict authority prototypes for schools and classrooms have the appeasing quality of an annual family ritual: There is a confirmation that time goes by while the important structures remain the same. The dissenters—using *rightly wrong* arguments—appear to be offering starkly polarizing pedagogical ideas that give the false impression of a debate that could bring educational progress, while ignoring not only the way schools are organized, but also fundamentally what is offered in classrooms. For *rightly wrong* thinkers—who believe that learning should be organized by the CONDUIT and EMPTY VESSEL metaphors and the homogeneous, strict authority prototype—schools are hierarchical structures, well organized by solid bricks of knowledge and glued together by the mortar of authority. The main ideological differences are too often just in the content of the bricks, such as Western canon versus ethnic studies, but with the same top-down hierarchy of authority. Similarly, planning and all key decisionmaking and power are at the top of the pyramid, respecting the established ideas of important voices—be they federal, state, or local authorities in agreement with the heads of corporations, religious leaders, and the latest "in" educational opinion makers. Although this top-down authority structure may appear rational and efficient, in practice this system has not worked well because, at a minimum, teaching is a complex activity that is hard to direct and improve from afar.

We do not believe that an ardent defense of the concept of public education excludes the need to recognize that there are private schools and also charter schools that have shown important results. In our perspective, good schools—whether private, charter, or traditional—have common features: explicit goals focusing on learning, capable and expert teachers, good working and collaborative conditions, longer and more diversified learning times and spaces, and regular systems of formative assessment to reflect on what's working with the students in order to plan for continuing improvements. Pedagogically, these strategies work whether the school is public or private, but not without the assistance of other agencies and social interventions. Schools and teachers alone cannot systematically and consistently overcome the negative impacts of poverty in children's learning in and outside educational institutions.

We want to emphasize this last point once again: Better learning demands that students and their families have access to the resources and supports needed to do the difficult work of constructing knowledge. This means not just in school but also in their homes and community. Learning modeled by GROWTH treats classrooms as complementary to home and community learning opportunities. As we have stated throughout the book, FREEDOM is the ability to do things and that ability requires support, more than being left on our own.[6]

A more comprehensive understanding of the metaphors and prototypes presented both by "our side" and by any "other side" does not automatically change how one feels about each side's argument. However, this knowledge is a very good way to assist us in clarifying our own thinking. Knowing the fundamental elements and logic underlying different education models enables us to understand better the relationships between conscious arguments and our automatic ways of thinking, including limits on the conscious altering of existing metaphor- and prototype-based understandings.

Lastly, embodied cognition is based on a *realistic* understanding of how people construct their subjectivities, because it recognizes the importance of unconscious, automatic ways of understanding as well as the relevance and limits of conscious rationality. Our interpretation of rationality in the context of education policy and practice offers scholars, policymakers, and practitioners better and more useful conceptual and pedagogical tools to overcome the limitations of the CONDUIT and EMPTY VESSEL–based models of education that go beyond simplistic dualistic battles of "good" versus "evil" and "efficiency" versus "caring" perspectives. Paraphrasing George Lakoff (2008), embodied cognition can be used as a 21st-century pedagogical tool to help us solve our 21st-century educational problems.

If we are ever to get education to work consistently for all Americans, it is essential that education policies and practices be based on accurate and realistic understandings of how people learn. Our goal in this book was to pull back the curtain on the idealistic and inaccurate notions about learning that dominate most of our current educational policies and practices, as well as the debates and reforms, and to offer some guidance, examples, and tools for how to better identify and advocate for more effective ones.

We are aware of the limitations of our approach. We do not believe there is a single, perfect pedagogical tool that will magically solve all the educational problems. That would be impossible. Our approach must be used in concert with other activities, both in and out of education. Still, we are hopeful that we have offered more realistic, research-based conceptual tools and guiding principles to detect the MADness of *rightly wrong* thinking and ineffective pedagogical projects. It is urgent to try better pedagogical alternatives and not to keep doing what has been shown to produce bad results. By now, we have experienced more than 20 years of educational reforms based on punishing standardized testing, curriculum simplification, and sustained blaming of public school teachers and unions for the systemic failures of schools, while ignoring or even dismissing the effects of poverty and inequality on learning opportunities. Such strategies, in the name of "high expectations" and "no excuses," have had the perverse effect of dumbing-down the educational landscape.

With this book, we are trying to find better ways of conveying the levels of complexity involved in our educational systems and explaining pedagogical alternatives to the current dumbing-down of schooling by going beyond telling redemptive stories of individual educational success against all odds. We all know somebody who exemplifies the redemptive power of schooling—a student who, in spite of multiple challenges, has worked hard, struggled with adversity and faithfully persisted, and thus benefitted from the current schooling model. There is nothing wrong with the protagonists of those stories—we all like and congratulate them. The problem is with the use and abuse of those stories as justification for maintaining the *rightly wrong* thinking of the status quo. These stories, while making us feel optimistic and good about the possibilities of individual success at schools, when used as the only and exclusive explanation at more systemic levels, are not very useful beyond bringing a sense of relief that encourages us to keep supporting a school system that produces nice redemptive individual stories, but doesn't actually work for the many.

We need to make an effort to resist the easy route of supporting *rightly wrong* ideas that make us feel good, but that do not maximize learning for most students, and we need to start experimenting and implementing strategies that may demand more effort and make us feel uncomfortable. If we don't start to do so, we will keep complaining about teachers, schools, students, parents, and superintendents, choosing new and old straw men to blame for our collective educational failures and finding comfort in the individual stories of school redemption. We hope that concerned parents, citizens, teachers, and policymakers use what we offer here to identify, promote, and implement ideas that are right and smart for maximizing learning for their own children and all our children.

Notes

Introduction

1. Taking the country as a whole (and we know that these types of comparisons are problematic), U.S. students are ranked near the bottom of industrialized nations on the most recent administration of the Programme for International Assessment (PISA). According to the 2012 results from the PISA, among 34 Organisation for Economic Co-operation and Development (OECD) countries, U.S. 15-year-olds ranked #26 in mathematics, #17 in reading, and #21 in science (OECD, 2013a, p. 1). Further, "Students in the United States have particular weaknesses in performing mathematics tasks with higher cognitive demands, such as taking real-world situations, translating them into mathematical terms, and interpreting mathematical aspects in real-world problems" (p. 1).

2. According to a 2013 *Education Week* analysis, the overall U.S. graduation rate in 2010 was nearly 75%, which is the highest rate since 1973 (Swanson & Lloyd, 2013).

3. Our understanding of *rationality* follows Lakoff's perspective (1987; 2008) among others (e.g., Ariely, 2008, 2010; Bechara, Damasio, Tranel, & Damasio, 2005; Damasio, 1994, 1999, 2003, 2010; Lakoff & Johnson, 1980/2003, 1999; Westen, 2007) in the sense that rationality, reasoning, and understanding can no longer be approached as a purely conscious activity, nor should rationality be idealized as such. Lakoff (2008) encourages researchers

> to embrace a deep rationality that can take account of, and advantage of, a mind that is largely unconscious, embodied, emotional, empathetic, metaphorical, and only partly universal. A New Enlightenment would not abandon reason, but rather understand that we are using real reason, shaped by our bodies and brains and interactions in the real world, reason incorporating emotion, structured by frames and metaphors and images and symbols [including prototypes], with conscious thought shaped by the vast and invisible realm of neural circuitry not accessible to consciousness. (pp. 13–14)

4. The opening sentence of Sasha Zucker's 2004 Policy Report for Pearson Education, Inc., entitled *Scientifically Based Research: NCLB and Assessment*, states, "A significant aspect of the *No Child Left Behind Act of 2001* (NCLB) is the use of the phrase 'scientifically based research' well over 100 times throughout the text of the law" (p. 2).

5. Kahneman (2011) also refers to fast thinking as "System 1" and slow thinking as "System 2."

6. In his *Education Week* article, Polikoff (2014) links to eight articles to support his position that "standards-based reform and accountability improve student outcomes" (para. 5), which he uses as support for his initial position (implied by the headline and opening paragraphs) that, by itself, "standards-based reform works" (para. 1). None of the eight linked articles addresses the impact of standards-based reform alone and none of the eight articles addresses standards-based reform as the primary reform effort being examined. All eight articles address the impact of one or more types of external accountability measures—No Child Left Behind sanctions, high-stakes testing, vouchers, and the stigma of low accountability grades for a school—as the driver of any improvements in student achievement measures, which were most often standardized test scores.

7. See www.nbpts.org/national-board-certification

8. The NBPTS provides an extensive list of research studies on the positive impact of National Board certified teachers on student achievement, which can be found at www.nbpts.org/promoting-student-learning-growth-achievement.

9. See the NBPTS webpage, *Who We Are*, at www.nbpts.org/nbpts-2013-01-08-nbct-student-achievement.

10. We do not support reductionist perspectives that operate from the principle that only that which can be counted counts as evidence, nor with the exclusive association of "scientific" educational research with "gold standard" quantitative models (Philips, 2014). We believe that such a limited view of empirical evidence can result in an overreliance on hewing to the data, resulting in flawed practices and broader misunderstandings of student learning and achievement, as well as what constitutes effective education policies (Dumas & Anderson, 2014; Donmoyer, 2014).

11. We see a similarity between our description of rightly wrong thinking and Economist Paul Krugman's use of the term "zombie idea" as the label for an idea that "should have been killed by evidence, but refuses to die" (2014, para. 3).

12. We find Haidt's early research on post hoc explanations for initial automatic conclusions for moral and emotional issues to be very compelling. However, we disagree with some of the subsequent conclusions expressed in Haidt (2012) regarding genetic predispositions for being liberal or conservative, and his conclusion that liberals have lesser moral sensibilities regarding

loyalty, authority, and sanctity as compared to conservatives. We agree with the critiques of these aspects of his work expressed by Churchland (2013) and Greene (2013).

13. According to Arbesman (2012) and Churchland (2013), the trumping of consciously examined facts by the automatic response of our unconscious mind is so common that it has a name, the Semmelweis Reflex. It is named after Hungarian physician Ignaz Semmelweis. In the mid-1800s, Semmelweis demonstrated that washing hands with chlorinated lime would disinfect them and reduce death by infection in patients. Unfortunately, his evidence was dismissed as absurd and even offensive by leading doctors of the day. As a result, handwashing by doctors did not become common practice until many years after Semmelweis's death.

Kahneman (2011) describes the initial tendency of "people (and scientists, quite often) [to] seek data that are likely to be compatible with the beliefs they currently hold" as Confirmation Bias (p. 81). Kahneman links the phenomenon of Confirmation Bias to the idea that our automatic mental process of "understanding a statement must begin with an attempt to believe it: You must first know what the idea would mean if it were true. Only then can you decide whether or not to *unbelieve* it" (p. 81, emphasis in original). Kahneman attributes this theory of automatic initial believing to Harvard psychologist Daniel Gilbert (Gilbert, Krull, & Malone, 1990).

Chapter 1

1. The subtitle for Hirsch's *Cultural Literacy* is "What every American needs to know," with an additional front cover statement on the "updated and expanded" edition that says, "Includes 5,000 essential names, phrases, dates, and concepts." Hirsch's Core Knowledge Sequence can be found at www.core-knowledge.org/mimik/mimik_live_data/view.php?id=1833&record_id=103

2. In 2002, Jerry Jesness published an article in *Reason* magazine entitled "Stand and Deliver Revisited." Jesness interviewed Escalante and many of the key players in the rise and fall of his calculus program at Garfield High School. The article is thorough and well worth reading in its entirety. It is available on-line at reason.com/archives/2002/07/01/stand-and-deliver-revisited.

Jesness describes several important points concerning how Escalante's success was different from what was portrayed in the movie. These points include the many years, not 1 year, that it took to enable the students to succeed in calculus; the need for a many-year system of math courses, including those at feeder middle schools, not just 1 or 2 years of math classes, to prepare students to succeed at calculus; and the assistance of other skilled math teachers as well as the support of the principal, not just a lone teacher fighting the system, to achieve the great success that began in Escalante's fifth year at Garfield High

School. Jesness concludes that Escalante's vision and dedication were key to the calculus program's success; however, once the supporting system began to come apart, the calculus program's level of success was reduced.

3. See, e.g., Dianne Leoni's *Educreations* website, which states (wrongly) how useful the butterfly algorithm is in *learning* how to add and subtract fractions: "Using a visual image, students can easily find the sums and differences of fractions. This method leaves a mental picture of the algorithm which can be effortlessly applied." Available at www.educreations.com/lesson/view/butterfly-method-addition-and-subtraction-of-fract/1242563/. We contend that practicing how to use the butterfly algorithm can be considered "learning" how to add and subtract fractions to the extent that learning does not extend to understanding why fractions work as they do and how to apply them to real and everyday situations.

4. Schooling organized around a Mechanistic/Industrial/Banking model was crucial in terms of progressively expanding access to formal education to most sectors of the population. We are not opposed to the notion of having large-scale educational systems, nor are we defending some sort of nostalgic and idealized small school system. Our criticism is structurally similar to those of Michael Apple (1990), Gert Biesta (2011), Samuel Bowles and Herbert Gintis (2011), Martin Carnoy and Henry Levin (1985), and especially Paulo Freire (1970/1993, 1994, 1998) regarding how the structuring of school systems follows ideological imperatives and the tensions emerging from a political logic (that of liberal democracies) and an economic logic (expanding forms of capitalistic production and distribution). Specifically, we are claiming that the ideological nature of the Mechanistic/Industrial/Banking model of schooling is built with a logic that, although it includes large numbers of potential students, does so by classifying them in a mechanistic way (there are "naturally" good and bad students), systematically ranking them in hierarchies of successful and unsuccessful students, and subjecting all learners to passively received preselected knowledge, as if deposits were being made into a bank.

Chapter 3

1. Due to page constraints and concerns about readability, we do not, for example, discuss directly or in much depth the concept of student and educator motivation or the relationship of motivation to learning, which are also key aspects of an effective educational system.

2. The *Private Universe* DVD and supplemental resources can be found at www.learner.org/resources/series28.html.

3. See the description of the practice habits of soccer star Lionel Messi, beginning on page 30 in Lemov et al. (2012).

4. See the description of the difference between drill (practicing individual discrete skills) and scrimmage (practicing the big picture of a full activity), beginning on page 54 in Turley, 2008.

5. According to Lakoff and Johnson (2003), we experience a gestalt understanding such that "the complex of [component] properties occurring together is more basic to our experience than their separate occurrence" (p. 71; emphasis in original).

6. We note that "choking" in the heat of the moment is the opposite of big-chunk gestalt thinking. When you "choke"—when you fail to do something at an especially important moment that you have done repeatedly before, even under pressure—your mind thinks about the task at hand in terms of its small steps rather than in the larger chunks of gestalt or forward models and so it becomes less efficient and effective (Bascom, 2012).

Chapter 4

1. As part of its effort to develop safe and supportive schools, the U.S. Department of Education's Office of Safe and Healthy Students funds the National Center on Safe Supportive Learning Environments (NCSSLE) to help schools and communities contend "with many factors that affect the conditions for learning, such as bullying, harassment, violence, and substance abuse" (Safe Supportive Learning website: About).

2. See, for example, the description of Finnish teacher preparation described by Pasi Sahlberg in his book *Finnish Lessons* (2012a) and his Stanford Research Brief, *The Secret to Finland's Success: Educating Teachers* (2010).

3. See the American Montessori Society, www.amshq.org/Montessori-Education.aspx; Rudolf Steiner College for Waldorf Teacher Education, www.steinercollege.edu/waldorf; Citizen Schools, www.citizenschools.org/about/education-reform/; and Performance Assessment teacher.scholastic.com/professional/assessment/perfassess.htm and scale.stanford.edu/student.

Chapter 5

1. Also see the *Public Policy Institute of California Statewide Survey*, on education at www.ppic.org/content/pubs/survey/S_413MBS.pdf.

2. See, for example, the video *Reclaiming the Promise*, created by the American Federation of Teachers, that describes common myths about education and the resulting wrongly targeted solutions. It is available at www.youtube.com/watch?v=hf9UVg-TdH0.

3. In reviewing the research on "skills-in-a-box" literacy solutions, Schoenbach, Greenleaf, and Murphy (2012) conclude that no matter what the

emphasis of a particular program, "repeated studies have demonstrated that isolated instruction in grammar, decoding, or even reading comprehension skills may have little or no transfer effect when students are actually reading" (p. 8). As a result of these studies and their own experience working with hundreds of teachers, Schoenbach et al. use a reading apprenticeship model of literacy development for students that is heavily dependent on training teachers to effectively manage the social, personal, cognitive, and knowledge-building dimensions that students use to develop strong reading comprehension skills.

4. We like how Robyn Jackson, Ph.D., describes the balance of teaching and learning in *Never Work Harder Than Your Students and Other Principles of Great Teaching* (2009), in which she describes effective teaching as enabling students to effectively do the hard work of learning.

5. We see a prime and almost ironic example of the idea that you cannot demand that people—even or perhaps especially scholars and researchers—learn something or change their minds in the linguistic debates that occurred between leaders in the field during the 1960s and 1970s. Randy Allen Harris describes the fierce, angry debates that occurred in his book *The Linguistic Wars* (1995).

6. Unfortunately, we need to do much more in this area. For example, *America's Report Card 2012* from Save the Children and First Focus gives the United States an overall grade of C- when it comes to providing the educational, economic, and social resources that students need to learn to a high level.

7. See the information and resources available on student and teacher performance assessment on the Stanford Center for Assessment, Learning, and Equity (SCALE) website at scale.stanford.edu/.

8. Bafa Bafa is a cross-cultural roleplay game where students are divided into two cultures that they learn and live in separate rooms. Representatives from each culture are sent to the other culture's room to learn through interaction and then report back to their home culture. The goal is to learn about how each culture works, often with funny and eye-opening results. For information and resources about Bafa Bafa, see www.stsintl.com/business/bafa.html.

9. See, for example, WestEd's SimScientists Human Body Systems simulations at www.wested.org/research_study/simscientists-human-body-systems-using-simulations-to-foster-integrated-understanding-of-complex-dynamic-interactive-systems/.

10. For additional discussion of the possible use of videogames in school or other educational settings with Arizona State University professor James Gee and University of Pennsylvania professor Angela Duckworth, see the *Education Week* article "Webinar: The Intersection of Video Games and Noncognitive Skills" (Herold, 2013), available at /blogs.edweek.org/edweek/DigitalEducation/2013/09/Webinar_intersection_video_games_noncognitive_skills.html.

11. For research-based information and resources on flipped classrooms, see *Flipping the Classroom* from Vanderbilt University's Center for Teaching (Brame, 2013).

12. See www.lindsay.k12.ca.us/District/Department/689-Performance-based-System.

13. Superintendent Tom Rooney regularly states how the Performance Based System is intended to meet the individual learning style and learning timeline of each student (personal communication). Author Eric Haas is working with the Lindsay Unified School District to help them implement their Performance Based System.

14. See www.lindsay.k12.ca.us/District/Department/386-Research-and-Evaluation/13187-Mindset.html.

15. Part of what makes teaching so difficult is that more effective teachers are not only experts in their knowledge of their discipline, but also experts in the common misconceptions of their students in that discipline and experts in the best pedagogical practices for enabling their students to construct more accurate and sophisticated understandings given their initial inaccurate and naïve understandings (see Sadler, Sonnert, Coyle, Cook-Smith, & Miller, 2013).

16. More information on the WRITE Institute program can be found at www.sdcoe.net/lls/english-learner/Pages/write-institute.aspx. Author Eric Haas is currently evaluating one of the WRITE Institute programs as principal investigator of an Institute of Education Studies (IES) grant, number R305A110176-13.

17. For more resources and discussion about the use of miscue analysis in the assessment of student reading abilities, see Ongoing Assessment for Reading by Jeanne Gunther (2013), and the associated links on the Learn NC website page at www.learnnc.org/lp/editions/readassess/2.0

18. Extensive information on what National Board Certification is and the process for how a teacher can become National Board certified can be found on the National Board for Professional Teaching Standards (NBPTS) website at www.nbpts.org/.

19. The NBPTS provides an extensive list of research studies on the positive impact of National Board certified teachers on student achievement, which can be found at www.nbpts.org/promoting-student-learning-growth-achievement.

Another example of teacher professional development that is based in part on the National Board Certification process is Stanford's Teaching Performance Assessment System (scale.stanford.edu/teaching).

20. See NCBT teacher resources at www.nbpts.org/candidate-mentoring

21. Extensive information about Teach for America (TFA) can be found on its website at www.teachforamerica.org/. Professor Diane Ravitch describes the TFA program and its results in her book *Reign of Error* (2013a). Also, Barbara Torre Veltri describes her experiences mentoring TFA teaching in *Learning on*

Other People's Kids: Becoming a Teach for America Teacher (2010), while TFA alum and staff member Victor Diaz describes the experiences of two individual TFA teachers and TFA in general in the book chapter, "Myth 13: Teach for America teachers are well trained, highly qualified, and get amazing results" (Berliner & Glass, 2014).

22. There are also non–peer-reviewed studies that have shown more positive TFA impacts on student achievement than the more rigorous studies referenced here (see, e.g., Clark et al., 2013; Xu, Hannaway, & Taylor, 2008). Both of these studies showed that TFA teachers outperformed the comparison high school teachers. However, the criticisms of the weaknesses of these studies (Heilig & Jez, 2010, 2014), including the Institute of Education Sciences' (IES) What Works Clearinghouse (2008) description of the limitations of the Xu et al. study, mean that the results of these non–peer-reviewed reports may be imprecise and misleading (Heilig & Jez, 2010, 2014). For the Xu et al. (2008) study, it was not always clear from the school and district records whether the teachers listed in the study as TFA teachers were actually TFA teachers (see description of the relationship between end of course proctors and actual course teachers, p. 9). In the Clark et al. (2013) study, it was not clear how TFA teachers compared to traditionally prepared and certified teachers because the teachers in the comparison group "could have entered teaching through either a traditional or less selective alternative route to certification" (p. xxi). It is important to note that the Xu et al. (2008) study was updated with one year of additional data and published in the peer-reviewed *Journal of Policy Analysis and Management* (Xu et al., 2011). However, the 2011 study contained the same methodological issues as the 2008 study that were criticized by the IES's What Works Clearinghouse (2008).

23. In the executive summary to their 2010 report, Heilig and Jez describe the overall research results on the impact of TFA teachers on student achievement and school improvement compared to other teachers this way:

> Research on the impact of TFA teachers produces a mixed picture, with results affected by the experience level of the TFA teachers and the group of teachers with whom they are compared. Studies have found that, when the comparison group is other teachers in the same schools who are less likely to be certified or traditionally prepared, novice TFA teachers perform equivalently, and experienced TFA teachers perform comparably in raising reading scores and a bit better in raising math scores.
>
> The question for most districts, however, is whether TFA teachers do as well as or better than credentialed non-TFA teachers with whom school districts aim to staff their schools. On this question, studies indicate that the students of novice TFA teachers perform significantly less well in reading and mathematics than those of credentialed beginning teachers.
>
> Experience has a positive effect for both TFA and non-TFA teachers. Most studies find that the relatively few TFA teachers who stay long enough to become

fully credentialed (typically after two years) appear to do about as well as other similarly experienced credentialed teachers in teaching reading; they do as well as, and sometimes better than, that comparison group in teaching mathematics. However, since more than 50% of TFA teachers leave after two years, and more than 80% leave after three years, it is impossible to know whether these more positive findings for experienced recruits result from additional training and experience or from attrition of TFA teachers who may be less effective.

From a school-wide perspective, the high turnover of TFA teachers is costly. Recruiting and training replacements for teachers who leave involves financial costs, and the higher achievement gains associated with experienced teachers and lower turnover may be lost as well.

Thus, a simple answer to the question of TFA teachers' relative effectiveness cannot be conclusively drawn from the research; many factors are involved in any comparison. The lack of a consistent impact, however, should indicate to policymakers that TFA is likely not the panacea that will reduce disparities in educational outcomes. (paras. 2–6).

24. Two examples of corporate support for TFA include a $20 million donation by the Walton Family Foundation (www.philanthropynewsdigest.org/news/walton-family-foundation-awards-20-million-to-teach-for-america) and donations from Subaru, FedEx, and J. Crew (see EduShyster [2013], at edushyster.com/?p=3795). By comparison, as noted above, the NBPTS just recently surpassed 100,000 National Board certified teachers over the course of its 30-year history.

25. As we described in Chapter 3, there are no shortcuts to expertise. Expecting inexperienced, barely trained teachers to have level 5 knowledge is a flaw in the logic of the TFA model. A further flaw is that the level 5 understanding that a teacher should have is something more than the level 4 understanding of an expert actor. This is why the most successful actors in a discipline are rarely the best teachers and coaches. Teachers must have the additional conscious knowledge of how to enable students to progress to the highest level of understanding, which is beyond—or at least different from—the knowledge of how to successfully act oneself. This difference between an expert actor and an expert teacher explains the different success of Michael Jordan and Larry Bird on one hand and Phil Jackson on the other. Michael Jordan and Larry Bird, two Hall of Fame basketball stars, won multiple MVP awards and NBA championships as players, but as coaches, neither one ever won an NBA championship or had one of their players win an MVP. In contrast, Phil Jackson, who was a solid NBA player serving mostly as a second-team substitute, won 11 NBA championships as the coach of two different teams. (See the Wikipedia information on the careers of Michael Jordan [en.wikipedia.org/wiki/Michael_Jordan], Larry Bird [en.wikipedia.org/wiki/Larry_Bird], and Phil Jackson [en.wikipedia.org/wiki/Phil_Jackson]. Note that although Larry Bird did not ever win an NBA championship as a coach, he was named Coach of the Year in 1998.)

26. See the previous discussions on both issues, including these references that address the relationship between student socioeconomic status and achievement (see, e.g., Berliner, 2009 & 2014; Borman & Dowling, 2006; Bowles & Gintis, 2011; Duncan & Murnane, 2011; Garcy, 2013; Lareau, 2000; Marder, 2012; OECD, 2013b) and the high levels of child poverty in the United States compared with other industrialized countries (see, e.g., First Focus & Save the Children, 2012).

27. In the Introduction, we described the lack of evidence in support of the notion that the implementation of any standards will result in greater or high levels of student achievement. For both the use of test scores in teacher evaluations and charter schools, there is strong evidence that, in and of themselves, they are ineffective at improving student achievement (see overviews in Berliner, Glass, & Associates, 2014; Paufler & Amrein-Beardsley, 2013; Ravitch, 2011, 2013a). Two studies by Stanford University's Center for Research on Education Outcomes (CREDO) found that charter schools perform about the same as or worse than public schools with similar demographics (2009, 2013). There is also consistent evidence that charter schools create greater segregation than neighboring public schools by including smaller percentages of students with special education needs and minority students (Cobb & Glass, 2003; Government Accountability Office, 2012; Institute on Metropolitan Opportunity, 2013; Institute on Race and Poverty, 2008). There is also strong evidence that the use of student test scores for teacher evaluations, often referred to as a Value-Added Model (VAM), is an unreliable indicator of teaching ability (see American Educational Research Association and National Academy of Education, 2011; Amrein-Beardsley et al., 2013; Baker et al., 2013; Darling-Hammond, 2010). For example, a study by Newton, Darling-Hammond, Haertel, and Thomas (2010) showed that teacher scores are highly unstable, with the same teacher's score varying by one to three deciles across classes, years, and evaluation models. A compelling example of the lack of stability in teacher evaluations based on student test scores comes from the Florida teacher Simone Ryals' description of being a state finalist for a presidential teaching award in 2012 (CBS Miami, 2012) and then being named as "an inferior teacher in need of serious improvement" in 2014 (Ryals, 2014, para. 6).

Chapter 6

1. The postcard with this saying was sent to one of the authors by one of his graduate students with the note, "Thanks for spending one wonderful scholarly semester trying to teach us what I learnt in 30 seconds reading this postcard!"

2. The students in this photograph are, from front to back, Ruby Baden-Lasar, Marquinho Oliveira, and Michaela Poynor-Haas, from Oakland, CA.

3. In an article comparing Finnish schools with U.S. schools, Pasi Sahlberg (2012b) quotes education scholar Michael Fullan about what makes Finnish schools better. Fullan implicitly dismisses the primary methods for change advocated by Michelle Rhee and her StudentsFirst organization:

Michael Fullan, a Canadian educational change scholar, speaks about "drivers of change," such as education policy or strategy levers, which have the best chances of driving intended change in education systems. "In the rush to move forward," writes Fullan, "leaders, especially from countries that have not been progressing, tend to choose the wrong drivers." "Wrong drivers" include accountability (vs. professionalism), individual teacher quality (vs. collegiality), technology (vs. pedagogy), and fragmented strategies (vs. systems thinking). The Finnish experience shows that a consistent focus on equity and shared responsibility—not choice and competition—can lead to an education system where all children learn better than they did before. (p. 27)

4. David Berliner, reflecting on the work of philosophers Denis Philips and Nicholas Burbules, argues that well-warranted thinking is what we look for to back up credible claims in education. Scientific claims in our field should offer more than a mere assertion, opinion, or belief; they need to offer *warranted* assertions, opinions, or beliefs. As Berliner (2013b) asserts, this distinction is quite important:

And this is where politicians and educational researchers differ. Too many politicians accept weak warrants for their own, or other people's beliefs, just as do many educators and the general population. What we need from the political apparatus in each of our countries is warranted policies. Unfortunately what we too often get is opinions, beliefs, and policy by anecdote. We need strong warrants for our policies and evaluations that are fitted to the complexity of what it is we are evaluating. That often requires valuing human judgment as much or more than quantitative methods. (p. 8)

5. Economists Erik Hanushek and Ludger Woessmann (2009) ask the question: What makes countries grow faster: more schooling or more knowledge and cognitive skills? Knowing more has a bigger impact at a macro level than more schooling.

6. For an excellent summary of the type of policies that could greatly contribute to these complementarities, see Berliner (2013a).

References

Adescope, O., Lavin, T., Thompson, T., & Ungerleider, C. (2010). A systematic review and meta-analysis of the cognitive correlates of bilingualism. *Review of Educational Research, 80*(2), 207–245.

American Educational Research Association & National Academy of Education. (2011). *Getting teacher evaluation right: A brief for policymakers*. Available at www.google.com/url?sa=t&rct=j&q=&esrc=s&source=web&cd=1&ved =0CCoQFjAA&url=http%3A%2F%2Fwww.educationminnesota.org%2 F~%2Fmedia%2F9B2A2B94C1B84B18B5F58748DDECF275.ashx&ei= VNgfU8XqNY2gogTer4LYDQ&usg=AFQjCNFPmcCbyp5230Bwcx2xfmu 3JLNDQ&sig2=hkUpDPx7iJNqp7nNOhCTzw&bvm=bv.62788935,d.cGU

American Federation of Teachers. (2013). *Reclaiming the promise*. Available at www.youtube.com/watch?v=hf9UVg-TdH0

Amrein-Beardsley, A., Collins, C., Polasky, S., & Sloat, E. (2013). Value-Added Model (VAM) research for educational policy: Framing the issue. *Education Policy Analysis Archives, 21*, 4. Available at dx.doi.org/10.14507/ epaa.v21n4.2013

Apple, M. W. (1990). *Ideology and curriculum* (2nd ed.). New York, NY: Routledge.

Arbesman, S. (2012). *The half-life of facts: Why everything we know has an expiration date*. New York, NY: Penguin.

Ariely, D. (2008). *Predictably irrational, revised and expanded edition: The hidden forces that shape our decisions*. New York: HarperCollins.

Ariely, D. (2010). *The upside of irrationality: The unexpected benefits of defying logic at work and at home*. New York: HarperCollins.

Arnold, K. (2010, February 18). Kelly gets psychological on winning. Available at irish.nbcsports.com/2010/02/18/kelly-gets-psychological-on-winning/

Bachtold, M. (2013). What do students "construct" according to constructivism in science education? *Research in Science Education, 43*(6), 2477–2496.

Baker, B., Oluwole, J., & Green III, P. (2013). The legal consequences of mandating high stakes decisions based on low quality information: Teacher

evaluation in the Race-to-the-Top era. *Education Policy Analysis Archives,
21*(5). Available at dx.doi.org/10.14507/epaa.v21n5.2013

Baker, P. (1991, April). Metaphors of mindful engagement and a vision of better
schools. *Educational Leadership, 48*(1), 32–35.

Baldassare, M., Bonner, D., Petek, S., & Shrestha, J. (2013). *PPIC statewide
survey: Californians & education.* San Francisco, CA: Public Policy Institute of California.

Banchero, S. (2014, March 10). Shaking up the classroom: Some schools scrap
age-based grade levels, focus on mastery of material. *The Wall Street Journal.* Available at online.wsj.com/news/articles/SB10001424052702304899
704579391101344310812

Baptist, K. W. (2002). The garden as metaphor for curriculum. *Teachers Education Quarterly, 29*(4), 19–37.

Bartels, L. (2002). Beyond the running tally: Partisan bias in political perceptions. *Political Behavior, 24,* 117–150.

Bascom, N. (2012). Brainy ballplayers: Elite athletes get their heads in the game.
Science News, 181(1), 22–30.

Bechara, A., Damasio, H., Tranel, D., & Damasio, A. (2005). The Iowa gam-
bling task and the somatic marker hypothesis. *Trends in Cognitive Science,
9,* 159–162.

Benard, B. (2004). *Resiliency: What we have learned.* San Francisco, CA:
WestEd.

Bennett, T. (2013). *Teacher proof: Why research in education doesn't always mean
what it claims, and what you can do about it.* New York, NY: Routledge.

Berendt, E. (2008). *Metaphors for learning: Cross-cultural perspectives.* Amsterdam, Netherlands: John Benjamins Publishing.

Berliner, D. (2002a). Educational research: The hardest science of all. *Educational Researcher, 31*(8), 18–20.

Berliner, D. (2002b). In search of warrant. In M. P. Wolfe & C. Pryor (Eds.), *The
mission of the scholar: Essays in honor of Nelson Haggerson* (pp. 53–63).
New York, NY: Peter Lang Publishers.

Berliner, D. (2009). *Poverty and potential: Out-of-school factors and school
success.* Boulder, CO: National Center for Educational Policy. Available at
nepc.colorado.edu/publication/poverty-and-potential

Berliner, D. (2013a). Effects of inequality and poverty vs teachers and schooling
on America's youth. *Teachers College Record, 116*(1). Available at www.
tcrecord.org/content.asp?contentid=16889

Berliner, D. C. (2013b, October 24–25). Politics and evaluation. *Seminário Diá-
logos Para A Democratização Da Escola Pública No Século XXI: Desafios
E Possibilidades.* Angra dos Reis, Rio de Janeiro, p. 8.

Berliner, D. (2014). Exogenous variables and value-added assessments: A fatal
flaw. *Teachers College Record, 116*(1), 1–31.

Berliner, D., Glass, G. V., & Associates. (2014). *50 myths and lies that threaten America's public schools: The real crisis in education.* New York, NY: Teachers College Press.

Bialystok, E., Craik, F.I.M., Grady, C., Chau, W., Ishii, R., Gunji, A., & Pantev, C. (2005). Effect of bilingualism on cognitive control in the Simon task: Evidence from MEG. *NeuroImage, 24,* 40–49.

Biesta, G. (2011). *Learning democracy in school and society.* Rotterdam, Netherlands: Sense Publishers.

Bilton, N. (2010). Replacing a pile of textbooks with an iPad. *New York Times.* Available at bits.blogs.nytimes.com/2010/08/23/replacing-a-pile-of-textbook-with-an-ipad/?_php=true&_type=blogs&_r=0

Borman, G. D., & Dowling, N. M. (2006). Longitudinal achievement effects of multiyear summer school: Evidence from the Teach Baltimore randomized field trial. *Educational Evaluation and Policy Analysis, 28*(1), 25–48.

Botha, E. (2009). Why metaphors matter in education. *South African Journal of Education, 29,* 431–444.

Bowles, S., & Gintis, H. (2011). *Schooling in capitalist America: Educational reform and the contradictions of economic life.* Chicago, IL: Haymarket Books.

Bracey, G. (2009). *The Bracey report on the condition of public education.* Boulder, CO: Education and the Public Interest Center; Tempe, AZ: Education Policy Research Unit. Available at epicpolicy.org/publication/Bracey-Report

Brame, C. J. (2013). *Flipping the classroom.* Vanderbilt University, Center for Teaching. Available at cft.vanderbilt.edu/teaching-guides/teaching-activities/flipping-the-classroom/

Brooks, J., & Brooks, M. (1993). *The case for constructivist classrooms.* Alexandria, VA: Association for Supervision and Curriculum Development.

Brown, P. C., Roediger, H., & McDaniel, M. (2014). *Make it stick: The science of successful learning.* Cambridge, MA: Belknap Press.

Cabanac, A., Perlovsky, L., Bonnoit-Cabanac, M., & Cabanac, M. (2013). Music and academic performance. *Behavioural Brain Research, 256*(1), 257–260.

Camerer, C., Loewenstein, G., & Prelec, D. (2005, March). Neuroeconomics: How neuroscience can inform economics. *Journal of Economic Literature, XLIII,* 9–64.

Carnoy, M., & Levin, H. M. (1985). *Schooling and work in the democratic state.* Palo Alto, CA: Stanford University Press.

CBS Miami. (2012). Tamarac teacher named state finalist for presidential award. Available at miami.cbslocal.com/2012/09/10/tamarac-teacher-named-state-finalist-for-presidential-award

Center for Research on Education Outcomes. (2009). *Multiple choice: Charter school performance in 16 states.* Palo Alto, CA: Stanford University.

Center for Research on Education Outcomes. (2013). *National charter school study.* Palo Alto, CA: Stanford University.

Chi, M., Roscoe, R., Slotta, J., Roy, M., & Chase, C. (2012). Misconceived causal explanations for emergent processes. *Cognitive Science, 36*, 1–61.

Churchland, P. (2013). *Touching a nerve: The self as brain.* New York, NY: W. W. Norton.

Clark, A. (2013). *Mindware: An introduction to the philosophy of cognitive science.* New York, NY: Oxford University Press.

Clark, M. A., Chiang, H., Silva, T., McConnell, S., Sonnenfeld, K., Erbe, A., & Puma, M. (2013). *The effectiveness of secondary math teachers from Teach For America and the Teaching Fellows Programs* (NCEE 2013-4015). Washington, DC: National Center for Education Evaluation and Regional Assistance, Institute of Education Sciences, U.S. Department of Education.

Clawson, L. (2013, January 7). Rhee's StudentsFirst grades education on ideology, not results. *Daily Kos.* Available at www.dailykos.com/story /2013/01/07/1177063/-Rhee-s-StudentsFirst-grades-education-on-ideology -not-results

Cobb, C., & Glass, G. V. (2003, April). *Arizona charter schools: Resegregating public education?* Paper presented at the annual meeting of the American Educational Research Association, Chicago, IL. Available at www.eric. ed.gov/contentdelivery/servlet/ERICServlet?accno=ED478058

Cole, M. (2010). What's culture got to do with it? Educational research as a necessarily interdisciplinary enterprise. *Educational Researcher, 39*(6), 461–470.

Common Core State Standards Initiative. (2014). *In the states.* Available at www.corestandards.org/in-the-states

Cranston, J. (2010). What do you mean your staff is like family? *McGill Journal of Education, 45*(3), 579–595.

Cuban, L. (2003). *Oversold and underused: Computers in the classroom.* Cambridge, MA: Harvard University Press.

Cuban, L. (2013a, June 21). Larry Cuban on school reform and classroom practice: iPads in Los Angeles and TCO. Available at larrycuban.wordpress. com/2013/06/21/ipads-in-los-angeles-and-tco/

Cuban, L. (2013b, October 30). Larry Cuban on school reform and classroom practice: The tomato harvester, the smart gun, and the age-grade school: reframing the problem. Available at larrycuban.wordpress.com/2013/10/30/ the-tomato-harvester-the-smart-gun-and-the-age-graded-school-reframing-the-problem/

Damasio, A. (1994). *Descartes' error: Emotion, reason, and the human brain.* New York: HarperCollins.

Damasio, A. (1999). *The feeling of what happens: Body and emotion in the making of consciousness.* New York: Harcourt.

Damasio, A. (2003). *Looking for Spinoza: Joy, sorrow, and the feeling brain.* New York: Harcourt.

Damasio, A. (2010). *Self comes to mind: Constructing the conscious brain.* New York: Pantheon.

Darling-Hammond, L. (1997). *The right to learn: A blueprint for creating schools that work.* San Francisco, CA: Jossey-Bass.

Darling-Hammond, L. (2006). *Powerful teacher education: Lessons from exemplary programs.* San Francisco, CA: John Wiley and Sons.

Darling-Hammond, L. (2010). *The flat earth and education: How America's commitment to equity will determine our future.* New York, NY: Teachers College Press.

Darling-Hammond, L., Holtzman, D. J., Gatlin, S. J., & Heilig, J. V. (2005). Does teacher preparation matter? Evidence about teacher certification, Teach for America, and teacher effectiveness. *Education Policy Analysis Archives, 13*(42). Available at epaa.asu.edu/epaa/v13n42/

Darling-Hammond, L., & Sykes, G. (2003). Wanted, a national teacher supply policy for education: The right way to meet the "highly qualified teacher" challenge. *Education Policy Analysis Archives, 11*(33). Available at epaa. asu.edu/epaa/v11n33/

Deasy, R. (2002). *Critical links: Learning in the arts and student academic and social development.* Washington, DC: Arts Education Partnership.

Demir, C. (2007). Metaphors as a reflection of middle school students' perceptions of school: A cross-cultural analysis. *Educational Research and Evaluation, 13*(2), 89–107.

Donmoyer, R. (2014). What if educational inquiry were neither a social science nor a humanities field? Revisiting Joseph Schawb's "The Practical" in the aftermath of the science wars. *Education Policy Analysis Archives, 22*(8). Available at dx.doi.org/10.14507/epaa.v22n8.2014

Dumas, M. J., & Anderson, G. (2014). Qualitative research as policy knowledge: Framing policy problems and transforming education from the ground up. *Education Policy Analysis Archives, 22*(11). Available at dx.doi. org/10.14507/epaa.v22n11.2014

Duncan, G. J., & Murnane, R. (Eds.). (2011). *Whither opportunity? Rising inequality, schools, and children's life chances.* New York, NY: Russell Sage Foundation.

EduShyster. (2013, December 8). Give the gift of excellence: 300 million ways to support Teach for America this holiday season. Available at edushyster. com/?p=3795

Erickson, F. (2014). Scaling down: A modest proposal for practice-based policy research in teaching. *Education Policy Analysis Archives, 22*(9). Available at dx.doi.org/10.14507/epaa.v22n9.2014

Ericsson, K. A., Krampe, R., & Tesch-Romer, C. (1993). The role of deliberate practice in the acquisition of expert performance. *Psychological Review, 100*(3), 363–406.

Feldman, F. (2008). *From molecule to metaphor: A neural theory of language.* Cambridge, MA: MIT Press.

First Focus & Save the Children. (2012). *America's report card 2012: Children in the U.S.* Washington, DC: Authors.

Fischman, G. E., & Diaz, V. D. (2013). Education without redemption: Ten reflections about the relevance of the Freirean Legacy. *Interamerican Journal of Education for Democracy, 4*(2), 70–87.

Fischman, G. E., & Haas, E. (2012). Beyond "idealized" citizenship education: Embodied cognition, metaphors and democracy. *Review of Research in Education, 36*(Education, Democracy and the Public Good), 190–217.

Fischman, G. E., & Tefera, A. A. (2014). Qualitative inquiry in an age of educationalese. *Education Policy Analysis Archives, 22*(7). Available at dx.doi.org/10.14507/epaa.v22n7.2014

Freire, P. (1993). *Pedagogy of the oppressed* (new rev. 20th-anniversary ed.). New York, NY: Continuum. (Original work published 1970)

Freire, P. (1994). *Pedagogy of hope.* New York, NY: Continuum.

Freire, P. (1998). *Pedagogy of freedom: Ethics, democracy, and civic courage.* Lanham, MD: Rowman & Littlefield.

Fullan, M. (2001). *The new meaning of educational change* (3rd ed.). New York, NY: Teachers College Press.

Gallup Poll. (2013). Education. Available at www.gallup.com/poll/1612/education.aspx

Garcy, A. M. (2013). The effects of health insurance coverage on the math achievement trajectories of school children in Yuma County, Arizona: Implications for education accountability policy. *Education Policy Analysis Archives, 21*(80). Available at epaa.asu.edu/ojs/article/view/1370

Gauvain, M. (2001). *The social context of cognitive development.* New York, NY: Guilford Press.

Gawande, A. (2011, October 3). Top athletes and singers have coaches. Should you? *New Yorker.* Available at www.newyorker.com/reporting/2011/10/03/111003fa_fact_gawande?currentPage=all

Gee, J. (2007). *What video games have to teach us about learning and literacy* (2nd ed.). New York, NY: Palgrave Macmillan.

Gibbs, R. W. (2008). *The Cambridge handbook of metaphor and thought.* New York, NY: Cambridge University Press.

Gilbert, D., Krull, D., & Malone, P. (1990). Unbelieving the unbelievable: Some problems in the rejection of false information. *Journal of Personality and Social Psychology, 59*, 601–613.

Ginges, J., Atran, S., Medin, D., & Shikaki, K. (2007). Sacred bounds on rational resolution of violent political conflict. *Proceedings of the National Academy of Sciences of the United States, 104* (18), 7357–7360.

Goffman, E. (1986). *Frame analysis: An essay on the organization of experience.* Boston, MA: Northeastern.

Gold, B., Kim, C., Johnson, N., Kryscio, R., & Smith, C. (2013). Lifelong bilingualism maintains neural efficiency for cognitive control in aging. *Journal of Neuroscience, 33*(2), 387–396.

Government Accountability Office. (2012). *Charter schools: Additional federal attention needed to help protect access for students with disabilities.* Washington, DC: Author.

Greene, J. (2013). *Moral tribes: Emotion, reason, and the gap between us and them.* New York, NY: Penguin.

Gunther, J. (2013). Ongoing assessment for reading: Miscue analysis. *Learning NC.* Available at www.learnnc.org/lp/editions/readassess/2.0

Haas, E. (2007a). *The framing of No Child Left Behind.* Berkeley, CA: Rockridge Institute. Available at www.cognitivepolicyworks.com/resource-center/education-policy-and-practice/the-framing-of-no-child-left-behind/

Haas, E. (2007b). *Framing education: Why does NPR repeat the conservative production model?* Available at www.cognitivepolicyworks.com/resource-center/education-policy-and-practice/conservative-production-model/

Haas, E. (2008, January 13). *Students are like plants, not widgets.* Berkeley, CA: Rockridge Institute. Available at www.cognitivepolicyworks.com/resource-center/education-policy-and-practice/students-are-like-plants-not-widgets/

Haas, E., & Fischman, G. E. (2010). Nostalgia, entrepreneurship, and redemption: Understanding prototypes in higher education. *American Educational Research Journal-SIA, 47*(3), 532–562.

Haas, E., & Poynor, L. (2005). Issues of teaching and learning. In F. English (Ed.), *Handbook of educational leadership* (pp. 483–506). Thousand Oaks, CA: SAGE.

Haidt, J. (2006). *The happiness hypothesis: Finding modern truth in ancient wisdom.* New York, NY: Basic Books.

Haidt, J. (2012). *The righteous mind: Why good people are divided by politics and religion.* New York, NY: Pantheon.

Haier, R., & Jung, R. (2008). Brain imaging studies of intelligence and creativity: What is the picture for education. *Roeper Review, 30*, 171–180.

Hakuta, K., Santos, M., & Fang, Z. (2013). Challenges and opportunities for language learning in the context of the CCSS and the NGSS. *Journal of Adolescent & Adult Literacy, 56*(6), 451–454.

Hanushek, E. A., & Woessmann, L. (2009). *Do better schools lead to more growth? Cognitive skills, economic outcomes, and causation.* Discussion Paper No. 4575. Institute for the Study of Labor (IZA).

Harris, R. A. (1995). *The linguistic wars.* New York, NY: Oxford University Press.

Heath, C., & Heath, D. (2010). *Switch: How to change things when change is hard.* New York, NY: Crown Publishing Group.

Heilig, J. V., & Jez, S. J. (2010). *Teach for America: A review of the evidence.* East Lansing, MI: The Great Lakes Center for Education Research and Practice.

Heilig, J. V., & Jez, S. J. (2014). *Teach for America: Return to the evidence.* Boulder, CO: National Education Policy Center. Available at nepc.colorado .edu/publication/teach-for-america-return

Hernandez, M., Costa, A., Fuentes, L. J., Vivas, A. B., & Galles, N. S. (2010). The impact of bilingualism on the executive control and orienting networks of attention. *Bilingualism: Language and Cognition, 13*(3), 315–325.

Herold, B. (2013, September 26). Digital education: Webinar: The intersection of video games and noncognitive skills. *Education Week.* Available at blogs.edweek.org/edweek/DigitalEducation/2013/09/Webinar_intersection _video_games_noncognitive_skills.html

Hirsch, E. D. (1987). *Cultural literacy: What every American needs to know.* New York, NY: Vintage.

Hirsch, E. D. (2009). *The making of Americans: Democracy and our schools.* New Haven, CT: Yale University Press.

Howell, W. S. (1986). *The empathic communicator.* Long Grove, IL: Waveland Press.

Iacaboni, M. (2008). *Mirroring people: The new science of how we connect with others.* New York, NY: Farrar, Straus and Giroux.

Institute on Metropolitan Opportunity. (2013). Charter schools in the Twin Cities: 2013 update. Minneapolis, MN: Author. Available at www.law. umn.edu/uploads/16/65/1665940a907fdbe31337271af733353d/Charter-School-Update-2013-final.pdf

Institute on Race and Poverty. (2008). Failed promises: Assessing charter schools in the Twin Cities. Minneapolis, MN: Author. Available at www.law.umn.edu/ uploads/5f/ca/5fcac972c2598a7a50423850eed0f6b4/8-Failed-Promises -Assessing-Charter-Schools-in-the-Twin-Cities.pdf

Jackson, R. (2009). *Never work harder than your students and other principles of great teaching.* Alexandria, VA: Association for Supervision and Curriculum Development.

Jesness, J. (2002, July). *Stand and Deliver* revisited: The untold story behind the famous rise—and shameful fall—of Jaime Escalante, America's master math teacher. *Reason.* Available at reason.com/archives/2002/07/01/ stand-and-deliver-revisited/1

Kahan, D., Peters, E., Dawson, E. C., & Slovic, P. (2013). *Motivated numeracy and enlightened self-government.* Yale Law School Public Law Working Paper No. 307. New Haven, CT: Yale University.

Kahneman, D. (2011). *Thinking, fast and slow.* New York, NY: Farrar, Straus and Giroux.

Karafiath, B. L., & Brewer, J. (2013). It's a good thing more people don't care about global warming: A surprising journey into the world of memes. Available at www.slideshare.net/culture2inc/climatememe1

Kliebard, H. M. (1975). Metaphorical roots of curriculum design. In W. Pinar (Ed.), *Curriculum theorizing: The reconceptualists.* (pp. 84–85). Berkeley, CA: McCutchan.

Krall, R. M., Lott, K., & Wymer, C. (2009). Inservice elementary and middle school teachers' conceptions of photosynthesis and respiration. *Journal of Science Teacher Education, 20,* 41–55.

Krizman, J., Marian, V., Shook, A., Skoe, E., & Kraus, N. (2012). Subcortical encoding of sound is enhanced in bilinguals and relates to executive function advantages. *Proceedings of the National Academy of Science* [electronic version]. Available at www.pnas.org/content/early/2012/04/23/1201575109.full.pdf

Krugman, P. (2014, March 30). Jobs and skills and zombies. *New York Times.* Available at www.nytimes.com/2014/03/31/opinion/krugman-jobs-and-skills -and-zombies.html?_r=0

Kumashiro, K. (2008). *The seduction of common sense: How the right has framed the debate on America's schools.* New York, NY: Teachers College Press.

Kumashiro, K. (2012). *Bad teacher! How blaming teachers distorts the bigger picture.* New York, NY: Teachers College Press.

Lakoff, G. (1987). *Women, fire, and dangerous things: What categories reveal about the mind.* Chicago, IL: University of Chicago Press.

Lakoff, G. (2002). *Moral politics: How liberals and conservatives think* (2nd ed.). Chicago, IL: University of Chicago Press.

Lakoff, G. (2006a). Response to Steven Pinker: Defending freedom. *New Republic Online.* Available at www.powells.com/biblio?show=HARDCOVER :NEW:0374158282:23.00&page=authorsnote#page

Lakoff, G. (2006b). *Thinking points: Communicating our American values and vision.* New York, NY: Farrar, Straus and Giroux.

Lakoff, G. (2007). *Whose freedom? The battle over America's most important idea.* New York, NY: Picador.

Lakoff, G. (2008). *The political mind: Why you can't understand 21st-century American politics with an 18th-century brain.* New York, NY: Viking.

Lakoff, G., & Johnson, M. (1999). *Philosophy in the flesh: The embodied mind and its challenge to western thought.* New York, NY: Basic Books.

Lakoff, G., & Johnson, M. (2003). *Metaphors we live by.* Chicago, IL: University of Chicago Press. (Originally published 1980)

Lakoff, G., & Smith, G. W. (2012, August 22). *Romney, Ryan, and the Devil's budget: Will America keep its soul?* Available at www.huffingtonpost.com/ george-lakoff/romney-ryan-and-the-devil_b_1819652.html

Lareau, A. (2000). *Home advantage: Social class and parental intervention in elementary education.* New York, NY: Rowman & Littlefield.

LeDoux, J. (1999). *The emotional brain: The mysterious underpinnings of emotional life.* New York, NY: Touchstone.

LeDoux, J. (2003). *Synaptic self: How our brains become who we are.* New York, NY: Penguin.

Lemov, D., Woolway, E., Yezzi, K., & Heath, D. (2012). *Practice perfect: 42 rules for getting better at getting better.* San Francisco, CA: Jossey-Bass.

Levitin, D. (2007). *This is your brain on music: The science of a human obsession.* New York, NY: Penguin.

Liebow, E., Dominguez, V. R., Peregrine, P. N., McCarty, T. L., Nichter, M., Nardi, B., & Leeman, J. (2013). On evidence and the public interest. *American Anthropologist, 115*(4), 642–655.

Lindon, J. (2013). *Reflective practice and early years professionalism* (2nd ed.). London: Bookpoint Ltd.

LoPresto, M., & Murrell, S. (2011). An astronomical misconceptions survey. *Journal of College Science Teaching, 40*(5), 14–23.

Luke, A., Green, J., & Kelly, G. J. (2010). What counts as evidence and equity? *Review of Research in Education, 34,* pp. vii–xvii. Available at DOI: 10.3102/0091732X09359038

Marder, M. (2012). Failure of U.S. public secondary schools in mathematics. *Journal of Scholarship and Practice, 9*(1), 8–25.

May, G. L., & Short, D. (2003). Gardening in cyberspace: A metaphor to enhance online teaching and learning. *Journal of Management Education, 27*(6), 673–693.

Mechelli, A., Crinion, J., Noppeney, U., O'Doherty, J., Asburner, J., Frackowiak, R., & Price, C. J. (2004). Brief communications: Structural plasticity in the bilingual brain. *Nature, 431,* 757.

Mehta, J. (2013). *The allure of order: High hopes, dashed expectations, and the troubled quest to remake American schooling.* New York, NY: Oxford University Press.

Milton, J., Small, S. L., & Solodkin, A. (2004). On the road to automatic: Dynamic aspects in the development of expertise. *Journal of Clinical Neurophysiology, 21,* 134–143.

Milton, J., Solodkin, A., Hlustik, P., & Small, S. L. (2007). The mind of expert motor performance is cool and focused. *NeuroImage, 35,* 804–813.

Murphy, G. L. (2002). *The big book of concepts.* Cambridge, MA: MIT Press.

Nater, S., & Gallimore, R. (2006). *You haven't taught until they have learned: John Wooden's teaching principles and practices.* Morgantown, WV: Fitness Information Technology.

National Board for Professional Teaching Standards. (2013a). Programs. Available at www.nbpts.org/national-board-certification

National Board for Professional Teaching Standards. (2013b). Who we are. Available at www.nbpts.org/nbpts-2013-01-08-nbct-student-achievement

National Center for Education Statistics. (2013b). NAEP state profiles. Available at nces.ed.gov/nationsreportcard/states/

National Center on Safe Supportive Learning Environments (NCSSLE). (2014). About. Available at safesupportivelearning.ed.gov/about

National Research Council. (2008). *Assessing accomplished teaching: Advanced-level certification programs.* Washington, DC: The National Academies Press.

New Mexico Higher Education Department. (2014). *Report to the legislative finance committee: College readiness.* Report Number 14-02. Available at www.nmlegis.gov/lcs/lfc/lfcdocs/perfaudit/Higher%20Education%20Department%20-%20College%20Readiness.pdf

Newton, X., Darling-Hammond, L., Haertel, E., & Thomas, E. (2010). Value-added modeling of teacher effectiveness: An exploration of stability across models and contexts. *Educational Policy Analysis Archives, 18*(23). Available at epaa.asu.edu/ojs/article/view/810

Nutley, S. M., Davies, H. T. O., & Smith, P. C. (Eds.). (2000). *What works? Evidence-based policy and practice in public services.* Bristol, UK: The Policy Press.

Nutley, S. M., Walter, I., & Davies, H. T. (2007). *Using evidence: How research can inform public services.* Bristol, UK: The Policy Press.

O'Brien, A. (2012, November 26). Administrators: The power of Academic Parent Teacher Teams. *Edutopia.* Available at www.edutopia.org/blog/academic-parent-teacher-teams-anne-obrien

Ohio Board of Regents. (2013). 2013 status of Ohio graduates remediation: Report by district. Available at www.ohiohighered.org/sites/ohiohighered.org/files/uploads/data/hs_transition/--2013-Ohio-Remediation-Report.pdf

Organization for Economic Co-operation and Development. (2013a). *Programme for International Assessment (PISA): Results from PISA 2012: Country Note: United States.* Paris, France: Author.

Organization for Economic Co-operation and Development. (2013b). *Time for the U.S. to reskill? What the survey of the adult skills says.* Paris, France: Author.

Paufler, N. A., & Amrein-Beardsley, A. (2013). The random assignment of students in elementary classrooms: Implications for value-added analyses and interpretation. *American Eduation Research Journal, 51*(2), 1–35. Available at vamboozled.com/wp-content/uploads/2013/10/2013AERJRandomVAM.pdf

Philips, D. C. (2014). Research in the hard sciences, and in very hard "softer" domains. *Educational Researcher, 43*(1), 9–11.

Pink, D. (2011). *Drive: The surprising truth about what motivates us*. New York, NY: Riverhead Books.

Polikoff, M. (2014, February 19). Why I am optimistic about standards-based reform. *Education Week*. Available at blogs.edweek.org/edweek/rick_hess_straight_up/2014/02/why_im_optimistic_about_standards-based_reform.html

Prinz, J. (2002). *Furnishing the mind: Concepts and their perceptual basis*. Cambridge, MA: MIT Press.

Private Universe. (1987). Produced by the Harvard-Smithsonian Center for Astrophysics, Science Education Department, Science Media Group. Available for purchase from Annenberg Learner at www.learner.org/resources/series28.html

Public Policy Institute of California. (2013). *PPIC Statewide Survey, Californians and Education*. San Francisco, CA: Author.

Ravitch, D. (2011). *The death and life of American School Review: How testing and choice are undermining education*. New York: Basic Books.

Ravitch, D. (2013a). *Reign of error: The hoax of the privatization movement and the danger to America's public schools*. New York, NY: Knopf.

Ravitch, D. (2013b, February 12). *Why is education talk so vacuous?* Available at dianeravitch.net/2013/02/12/why-is-education-talk-so-vacuous/

Reddy, M. (1979). The conduit metaphor: A case of frame conflict in our language about language. In A. Ortony (Ed.), *Metaphor and thought* (pp. 284–310). Cambridge, UK: Cambridge University Press.

Resmovits, J. (2012, February 24). Michelle Rhee's backers include Obama bundler billionaire, big Romney backer. *Huffington Post*. Available at www.huffingtonpost.com/2012/02/24/michelle-rhees-backers-in_n_1300146.html

Rogoff, B. (1990). *Apprenticeship in thinking: Cognitive development in social context*. New York, NY: Oxford University Press.

Rogoff, B. (1998). Cognition as a collaborative process. In D. Kuhn & R. S. Siegler (Eds.), *Handbook of child psychology: Cognition, perception, and language* (5th ed., pp. 679–744). New York, NY: Wiley.

Rosch, E. (1978). Principles of categorization. In E. Rosch & B. B. Lloyd (Eds.), *Cognition and categorization* (pp. 27–71). Hillsdale, NJ: Erlbaum.

Ruppert, S. (2006). *Critical evidence: How the arts benefit student achievement*. Washington, DC: National Assembly of State Arts Agencies.

Ryals, S. (2014). I'm one of the worst teachers in my state. *Salon.com*. Available at www.salon.com/2014/03/31/im_one_of_the_worst_teachers_in_my_state

Sadler, P., Sonnert, G., Coyle, H., Cook-Smith, N., & Miller, J. L. (2013). The influence of teachers' knowledge on student learning in middle school physical science classrooms. *American Educational Research Journal, 50*(5), 1020–1049.

Sahlberg, P. (2010). *The secret to Finland's success: Educating teachers.* Stanford Center for Opportunity Policy in Education: Research Brief. Palo Alto, CA: Stanford University. Available at edpolicy.stanford.edu/sites/default/files/publications/secret-finland's-success-educating-teachers.pdf

Sahlberg, P. (2012a). *Finnish lessons: What can the world learn from educational change in Finland?* New York, NY: Teachers College Press.

Sahlberg, P. (2012b, Spring). A model lesson: Finland shows us what equal opportunity looks like. *American Educator,* 20–40.

Sahlberg, P. (2012c). Quality and equity in Finnish schools. *School Administrator,* 8(69), 27–30.

Sahlberg, P. (2013, May 15). What if Finland's great teachers taught in U.S. schools? *Washington Post.* Available at www.washingtonpost.com/blogs/answer-sheet/wp/2013/05/15/what-if-finlands-great-teachers-taught-in-u-s-schools-not-what-you-think/?print=1

Sawchuk, S. (2014, January 15). In strong Common Core endorsement, NEA and firm unveil curricula by "master teachers." *Education Week.* Available at blogs.edweek.org/edweek/teacherbeat/2014/01/nea_and_firm_unveil_curricula.html

Sawyer, K. (2011). The cognitive neuroscience of creativity: A critical review. *Creativity Research Journal,* 23(2), 137–154.

Schoenbach, R., Greenleaf, C., & Murphy, L. (2012). *Reading for understanding: How Reading Apprenticeship improves disciplinary learning in secondary and college classrooms.* San Francisco, CA: WestEd.

Schulz, K. (2010). *Being wrong: Adventures in the margins of error.* New York, NY: HarperCollins.

Sfard, A. (2009). Metaphors in education. In H. Daniels, H. Lauder, & J. Porter (Eds.), *Educational theories, cultures, and learning: A critical perspective* (pp. 39–50). New York, NY: Routledge.

Shanton, K. D., & Valenzuela, T. C. (2005). Not in the script: The missing discourses of parents, students, and teachers about Success For All. In L. Poynor & P. M. Wolfe (Eds.), *Marketing fear in America's public schools: The real war on literacy* (pp. 111–132). Mahwah, NJ: Lawrence Erlbaum Associates.

Shenker-Osorio, A. (2012). *Don't buy it: The trouble with talking nonsense about the economy.* New York, NY: PublicAffairs.

Smagorinsky, P., Jakubiak, C., & Moore, C. (2008). Student teaching in the contact zone: Learning to teach amid multiple interests in a vocational English class. *Journal of Teacher Education,* 59(5), 442–454.

Stanford Center for Assessment, Learning, and Equity (SCALE). (2013). Assessment system. Available at scale.stanford.edu/student/assessment-system

Stein, M., Larrabee, T., & Barman, C. (2008). A study of common beliefs and misconceptions in physical science. *Journal of Elementary Science Education,* 20(2), 1–11.

Strauss, V. (2013, January 7). Michelle Rhee's new state reform report card. *Washington Post*. Available at www.washingtonpost.com/blogs/answer-sheet/wp/2013/01/07/michelle-rhees-new-state-reform-report-card/

StudentsFirst. (2013). State of education: State policy report card 2013. Sacramento, CA: Author. Available at http://edref.3cdn.net/9e8505b2c4ad5ec0e8_u6m6ikky8.pdf

StudentsFirst. (2014). State of education: State policy report card 2014. Sacramento, CA: Author. Available at reportcard.studentsfirst.org/assets/2014NationalReport.pdf

Sullivan, F. R. (2011). Serious and playful inquiry: Epistemological aspects of collaborative creativity. *Educational Technology & Society, 14*(1), 55–65.

Swanson, C. B., & Lloyd, S. C. (2013). Nation's graduation rate nears a milestone. *Education Week*. Available at www.edweek.org/ew/articles/2013/06/06/34analysis.h32.html?intc=EW-DC13-LNAV

Teach for America. (2014). Our history. Available at www.teachforamerica.org/our-organization/our-history

Todorov, E. (2004). Optimality principles in sensorimotor control. *Nature Neuroscience, 7*, 907–915.

Truebridge, S. (2013). *Resilience begins with beliefs: Building on student strengths for success in school*. New York, NY: Teachers College Press.

Turley, S. (2008). Book review: You haven't taught until they have learned: John Wooden's teaching practices and principles. *Issues in Teacher Education, 17*(1), 102–107.

U.S. Department of Education. (2013). An innovative model for parent-teacher relationships. Available at www.ed.gov/oese-news/innovative-model-parent-teacher-partnerships

U.S. Department of Education. (2014). Office of safe and healthy students. Available at www2.ed.gov/about/offices/list/om/fs_po/oese/safehealth.html

Vandervoort, L. G., Amrein-Beardsley, A., & Berliner, D. C. (2004). National Board Certified Teachers and their students' achievement. *Education Policy Analysis Archives, 12*(46). Available at epaa.asu.edu/ojs/article/view/201

Varela, F., Thompson, E., & Rosch, E. (1991). *The embodied mind: Cognitive science and human experience*. Cambridge, MA: MIT Press.

Veltri, B. T. (2010). *Learning on other people's kids: Becoming a Teach for America teacher*. Charlotte, NC: Information Age Publishing.

Viorica, M., Anthony, S., & Schroeder, S. R. (2013). Bilingual two-way immersion programs benefit academic achievement. *Bilingual Research Journal, 36*(2), 167–186.

Walqui, A., & van Lier, L. (2010). *Scaffolding the academic success of adolescent English language learners: A pedagogy of promise*. San Francisco, CA: WestEd.

Westen, D. (2007). *The political brain: The role of emotion in deciding the fate of the nation.* Philadelphia, PA: Public Affairs.

What Works Clearinghouse. (2008). WWC quick review of the report "Making a difference? The effects of Teach For America in high school." Washington, DC: What Works Clearinghouse, U.S. Dept. of Education.

Whitehurst, G. (2009, October 14). *Don't forget curriculum.* Providence, RI: Brown Center Letters on Education, #3. Available at www.brookings.edu/papers/2009/1014_curriculum_whitehurst.aspx

Wincek, J. (1995). *Negotiating the maze of school reform: How metaphor shapes culture in a new magnet school.* New York, NY: Teachers College Press.

Wolford, G., Miller, M., & Gazzaniga, M. (2000). The left hemisphere's role in hypothesis formation. *Journal of Neuroscience, 20*(6), 1–4.

Xu, Z., Hannaway, J., & Taylor, C. (2008). *Making a difference: The effects of Teach for America in high school.* Available at www.urban.org/UploadedPDF/411642_Teach_America.pdf

Xu, Z., Hannaway, J., & Taylor, C. (2011). Making a difference? The effects of Teach For America in high school. *Journal of Policy Analysis and Management, 30*(3), 447–469.

Zucker, S. (2004). *Scientifically based research: NCLB and assessment.* Policy Report. San Antonio, TX: Pearson Education. Available at images.pearson-assessments.com/images/tmrs/tmrs_rg/ScientificallyBasedResearch.pdf?WT.mc_id=TMRS_Scientifically_Based_Research

Index

About the Authors

Eric M. Haas works with state and district departments of education by providing research and program evaluations. His research interests include the legal rights and education experiences of English learners, formative evaluation, and the process of policy change. His writings have appeared in books and peer-reviewed journals. Dr. Haas began his work in education as a Peace Corps Volunteer, teaching math and science in Liberia, West Africa.

Gustavo E. Fischman is professor in educational policy at the Mary Lou Fulton Teachers College, Arizona State University. His areas of specialization are comparative education and critical policy studies in education. Dr. Fischman has published extensively and presented in numerous national and international conferences, and has been a visiting scholar in graduate programs in Europe and Latin America. He is the lead editor of *Education Policy Analysis Archives* and *Education Review.*

Joe Brewer is co-founder and research director at Culture2 Inc., where he combines insights from complexity research, cognitive science, and cultural evolution to address major challenges confronting humanity. He works extensively with nonprofit organizations, government agencies, and social impact businesses to support the transition to planetary thriving.